You Can't Go *Wrong* By **Doing It Right**

50 Principles for Running A Successful Business

Stephen L. Goldstein

The Oasis Press®
Central Point, Oregon

You Can't Go Wrong By Doint It Right
Published by The Oasis Press®/PSI Research
© 1999 by Dr. Stephen L. Goldstein and Zada B. Phipps

All rights reserved. No part of this publication may be reproduced or used in any form or by any means, graphic, electronic or mechanical, including photocopying, recording, taping, or information storage and retrieval systems without written permission of the publishers.

This publication is designed to provide accurate and authoritative information in regard to the subject matter covered. It is sold with the understanding that the author and publisher are not engaged in rendering legal, accounting, or other professional service. If legal advice or other expert assistance is required, the services of a competent professional person should be sought.

> —from a declaration of principles jointly adopted by a committee of the American Bar Association and a committee of publishers.

Interior Designer and Editor: Lori Katz
Cover Designer: Steven Eliot Burns

Please direct any comments, questions, or suggestions regarding this book to:

>The Oasis Press®/PSI Research
>Editorial Department
>P.O. Box 3727
>Central Point, Oregon 97502-0032
>(541) 479-9464
>(541) 476-1479 fax
>*info@psi-research.com* e-mail

The Oasis Press® is a registered trademark of Publishing Services, Inc., an Oregon corporation doing business as PSI Research.

Library of Congress Cataloging-in-Publication Data
Goldstein, Stephen P., 1943–
   You can't go wrong by doing it right : principles for running a successful business / Stephen P. Goldstein.
     p. cm. - - (Success series)
   Includes bibliographical references and index.
   ISBN: 1-55571-490-0 (paper)
   1. Burdines (Department store) - - History. 2. Department stores - - Florida - - History. 3. New business enterprises - - Management. 4. Small business - - Management.   I. Title.   II. Series.
HF5465.U6B874 1999
658 - - dc21   - - dc21
[658]   99-13349
                                                                         CIP

Printed and bound in the United States of America
First Edition 10 9 8 7 6 5 4 3 2 1

♻ Printed on recycled paper when available.

*This book is dedicated
to
Zada Burdine Phipps
Patricia B. Phipps
and
Zada Dutton Hooten,
all of whom
are the spirit of
the real Burdine legacy*

CONTENTS

Foreword v

Introduction vii

Part I: 50 Principles for Running
a Successful Business 1

Part II: The Burdine Success Story 203

Acknowledgements 237

Bibliographical Note 239

Foreword

Today, too many businesses in America have become monsters, bullies, and thugs. They abuse their customers, their employees, and the general public — and they routinely get away with it, because the system is rigged for them. In their relentless pursuit of the bottom line, businesses, especially retailers, have become cold, callous, and calculating at the expense of the very patrons that they are supposed to serve.

These days, no matter what sophisticated marketing and advertising techniques they may use, companies of every size have adopted a "take-it-or-leave-it; let the public be damned" attitude. They seem to suggest, "If you don't like what we have or how we treat you, somebody else will. We'll sell our merchandise, because it's the law of averages and there's really no place else to go."

Worse than their indifference, businesses have grown accustomed to treating people with outright contempt. "Step back folks you bother me": Robots answer telephones, giving callers menus of options and buttons to press but no personal interaction. What few live salespeople have survived downsizing might just as well be robots. They know little about sales and almost nothing about customer service.

In addition, in the reality of today's labor market, companies now enjoy the luxury of using their employees at will — hiring, firing, laterally transferring, or otherwise disposing of them with an eye to swelling their profits. Gone are the days when loyalty between a company and its employees counted for anything.

What's more, society as a whole somehow has been brainwashed into believing that the only appropriate goal of any company worth a place on a stock exchange is to wring the last drop of short-term profit out of its operations at all (even human) costs. A business, we now seem to agree, is to be evaluated only in terms of the equity of its shareholders; it has no responsibility to serve the consuming public, no interest greater than its own survival, and certainly no broad social place or responsibility. In trying to become ultra-profitable, American businesses have become insensitive to people's needs, scrooge-like caricatures of the best that every captain of industry can be.

Saddest of all, most of the buying public doesn't know any better. Several generations of Americans have grown up since these unsavory conditions have become the status quo. They have never experienced a time when things were different and better.

You Can't Go Wrong By Doing It Right is about The Golden Age of Retail — and business in general — in America. It is the story of a successful company that was able to balance its corporate head with a human heart, one that knew how to treat its employees and its customers and still remain profitable. It takes us back to a time when the world was caring and considerate and suggests that even if we cannot turn back the clock, we can learn something meaningful from the past. It is a contrarian's dream-come-true and a pragmatist's nightmare, suggesting that warm-and-fuzzy nostalgia, more than harsh, cold reality, actually has a great deal to teach us — and that we still have much to learn.

Introduction

50 Principles for Running a Successful Business

The 50 principles for running a successful business have grown out of an honest-to-goodness American success story, the history of a great business and the two men who built it. An epic, it takes place against the backdrop of two wars, begins in Mississippi and ends in Florida, spans a frontier of at least a thousand miles, and unfolds during a period of more than one hundred years. Together, the principles reveal a lost art of doing business, recalling a time when shrewd entrepreneurs were able to make a profit without selling their souls.

Keen businessmen who always kept their eyes on the bottom line, William Murrah Burdine, Sr. and his son Roddey, Sr. never were blinded by the mere pursuit of dollars and cents. They never went to college or business school and never formally studied marketing, accounting, strategic planning, or even retail sales, but they "wrote the book" on how to create a thriving business simply and directly out of the traditions and values they inherited and the day-to-day experiences of their lives. They came of age in the nineteenth century, during The Age of Experience, when people's character and conduct more than their formal education and training shaped their lives, what they did, and whether they merely scraped by, excelled, or flat out failed.

William discovered how to start a successful business from scratch. He had the fire in his belly that excites and characterizes every successful first-generation entrepreneur, a self-actualizing passion, a willingness to risk everything, and an unstoppable determination to excel. He could identify a market just by instinct, without the benefit of a formally researched market survey. He also knew how to sell. And perhaps more important than anything else, he knew how to relate to people — how to ingratiate himself with others, put them at ease, and inspire their confidence in him and in his business. He was a master at making acquaintances feel as though he had known them forever and friends understand that they truly were a part of his life. Roddey learned how to build upon his father's success and take it in new directions and to greater heights. Together, with an uncanny ability and consistency, they turned every situation in which they found themselves to their advantage and put in place the foundation for a corporation that has created one sensation after another for a century.

From its beginning in 1898, the success of Burdines Department Store, in Miami, Florida, which William Murrah Burdine founded, has been the result of guts, grit, vision, finesse, one-upmanship, showmanship, staying power, just plain salesmanship, and a host of other energies that father and son exhibited and inspired in others. As a result of William's and his son's early efforts, for a century, Burdines has been as natural a part of the lush landscape as sunshine, the ocean, and palm trees. It is one of the oldest and most respected businesses in Florida. The footprints of its more than forty-five branches now extend into every community around the state.

In addition, because Burdines began in one of the world's leading tourist meccas, it has made a name for itself nationally and internationally, as people who visit Florida carry tales about it around the world. And routinely, as its buyers have circled the globe, word of Burdines' sub-tropical sophistication has traveled as well. Eventually, it set the pace for certain fashions even outside of its geographical region as naturally as it bested its competition at home.

Burdines always has been a financial success. Even during the Great Depression it remained fiscally sound. To this day, its corporate vital statistics are dizzying and enviable in dollars and sales, net profit and growth. It has long been the jewel in the crown of Federated Department Stores, to which it now belongs.

But beyond cold, impersonal numbers, Burdines always has been more than just a place of business; it has been an institution, possessed of a palpable, but indefinable, something that sets it apart from other stores. For some people, shopping or working at Burdines has been a way of life. To the degree that a corporation can be personified, Burdines has seen itself and has been thought of as everybody's friend or family member. It has been a pervasive influence in the lives of literally millions of men, women, and children. Everyone knows Burdines, has shopped there, and has a story to tell about the store that somehow, mysteriously, is more than just a place to shop.

All of the fame and glory that Burdines has attained for a century belie its humble, even primitive, beginnings, however. Unlike the overnight business wonders of today, the store did not spring full blown from a posh executive boardroom with the fanfare of some dramatically unveiled strategic plan, nor was it the product of a rapacious merger, acquisition, corporate raid, or hostile takeover. Instead, Burdines, the corporate giant, began as a mere trading post in the mosquito-infested mangroves of Miami during the frenzy of the Spanish-American War. It came about the old-fashioned way — from the heart and on a wing and a prayer. It was the result of one man's initial act of faith.

Ultimately, the question this story asks is "Why were the Burdines so successful in business? Did they have a magic formula?" Other companies and individuals had similar or even greater opportunities at the very same time that Burdines was coming into its own, but they failed. Even after Burdines was sold to Federated Department Stores in 1956 and passed out of family control, it retained a certain mystique. What was it about Burdines that made it different?

One Burdines president, George Whitten, summed up the company's success formula in three principles: "Treat people right, give them value for their money, and make your business an integral part of your community — that's the secret."

In the view of writer Maurice LaBelle, "The Burdine family left an indelible imprint on the history of Miami," because it "established excellence that became a standard for the Miami business community." Without a doubt, the general perception of Burdines as a business and the Burdines as people and business leaders was that they set an example for others to follow in everything that they did.

Both George Whitten's and Maurice LaBelle's perceptions are at least partially right, but there is much more to the Burdines' success formula than either of them observed. To begin with, it was a blend of three traditions. First of all, it was quintessentially Southern, reflecting the mild and humane traditions of the Old South. Second, it was thoroughly Victorian — formal yet personal, private but social, at once restrained and gracious. And finally, it was uniquely Burdine, the result of their special experiences and circumstances in life.

As a direct result of the special mix of their traditions, they never pursued the bottom line at the expense of everything else, though they never lost sight of the fact that they were in business to make a profit. The success that they achieved cannot be told just in cold numbers — the numbers of stores they built, the ever-increasing quantities of customers they served, and the rise in gross and net sales and profit over the years. In their way of doing business, *how* a company did business was at least as important as the results it produced.

The Burdine success formula in full was never written down or even alluded to by any of the family members. Modest in every way, they would never have presumed to codify the principles according to which they achieved their prosperity. And guarded beyond outward congenial appearances, they would not have been quite so foolish as to share all parts of their recipe with the competition. The closest they themselves came to expressing their success formula was a brief but telling corporate credo designed to motivate their own employees:

"The Burdine Creed"

To be first with the best and newest
To be honest in purpose and fair in business
To be ever watchful for ways to serve you better
To recognize and accept our responsibilities
to community, customers and employees
To keep our vision steady, our growth sound
To merit your friendship and confidence
by the quality of our service and merchandise

In fact, there were no fewer than 50 success principles by which the Burdines did business, a compendium of timeless, good practices valid in any commercial or professional enterprise, and even in life.

Looking back over the sum total of their actions during their years in business, it is possible to see a coherent and powerful index of how a company did run, could run, and even, perhaps, should run. It is an example of a lost art, part of a distant and too-often forgotten past that is available to, but beyond the everyday reach of, many people who could learn from the Burdine example.

Part I

50 Principles for Running a Successful Business

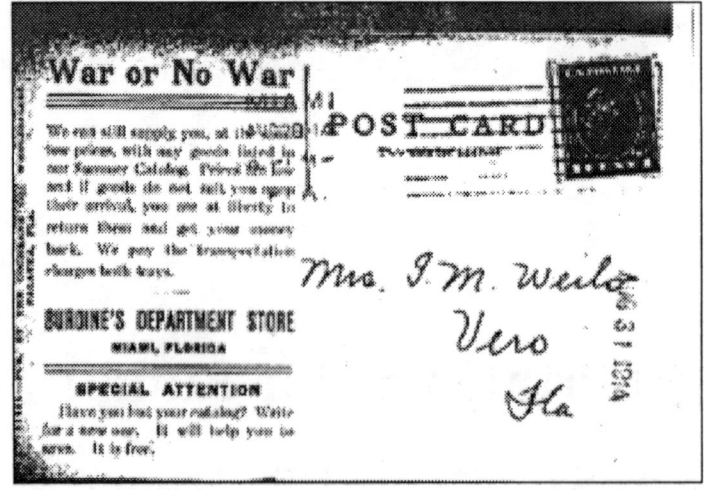

Burdines Archives

With a Victorian sense of grit and guts, Burdines always projected an indomitable image, a stiff upper lip — nowhere more resolutely than in this postcard dated August 31, 1914.

Supreme patriots, the Burdines nonetheless wanted all of their customers to know that nothing, not even the First World War, was going to stand between them, their patrons, and doing business.

❖ Success Principle 1

You've Gotta Have Grit, Guts, and Greed

Next to the strengths and defects in their gene pool, what people experience between the ages of eighteen and twenty-two often is responsible for the shape of the rest of their life. William Burdine spent those four years as a Confederate soldier during the Civil War, and they conditioned him to excel in business.

A wise Mississippian, Olivia Napoli observed that the generation of Southerners who survived the war and afterwards were successful in life were a different breed. They demonstrated a mixture of three important qualities — "grit, guts, and greed" — that enabled them not only to overcome adversity but to thrive in good times as well. The war had brought out their fortitude and courage, and it had left them with a wholesome "greed," a fire in the belly to get back everything that they had lost and had once taken for granted. They knew how to dig in, apply themselves, and get the job done at all costs.

Beneath the placid facade and courteous demeanor of William M. and Roddey Burdine were indomitable wills, which would not let anything stand in their way. In a pure example of Burdine family grit, in 1914, at the start of World War One, Burdines sent out a postcard to its customers, proclaiming that "War or No War," they were still in business and would still be guaranteeing delivery of their merchandise. This was not empty public relations bravado; it was an example of the resolve and determination which ran in their blood and with which they conducted their lives and their business. Deep down they believed that if they wanted to pursue a certain goal, nothing could, would, or should stop them.

Principle 1
You've Gotta Have Grit, Guts, and Greed

Applying this Principle to My Business Success

> **NEW DRY GOODS STORE**
>
> # W. M. Burdine & Son,
>
> Formerly of Bartow, have opened a first-class Dry Goods and Furnishing store in room joining the bank on the south. We carry a complete line of
>
> ## Dry Goods, Clothing, Shoes, Hats
>
> We make a specialty of
>
> ### Dress Goods, Trimmings, Laces,
> EMBROIDERY, BUTTONS, ETC.
>
> This department is presided over by Mrs. Quarterman, a lady of refined tastes and large experience in the business. She also has in her department, Lace Curtains, Table Linens, Sheetings, Bobinetts, Umbrellas, Hosiery, and Ladies' and Children's Fine Shoes. We take pride in our line of
>
> ## SHOES.
>
> We carry W. L. Douglass' and J. S. Nelson & Son's—Men's. Krippendorf - Dittman's, Plant & Mark's, and Carlisle Shoe Co.'s—Ladies', and Hill & Green's—Children's. These are all high-grade custom Shoes, and are unequaled in style and durability.
> In our introduction to the good people of Miami and Dade county, we will say that we expect, as in the past, to carry reliable, up-to-date goods and sell them as low as any reputable dealer. We expect by honorable, upright dealing, to merit a share of your patronage, as well as your good will. Yours to please,
>   W. M. BURDINE & SON.

Burdines Archives

Striking the first notes of a tone that would characterize its relations with the general public and its patrons for decades, Burdines' first ad in Miami in 1898 pledges its commitment to giving customers a fair deal: "We expect by honorable, upright dealing, to merit a share of your patronage, as well as your good will."

❖ Success Principle 2

Short-change Yourself Before You'd Cheat a Customer

Being successful in business is an art, not a science, and perfecting it is idiosyncratic and subjective. There is no single, foolproof formula that can guarantee the success of every enterprise. Everyone has to learn to take a little from here and there, to apply it, and then modify it as they see fit based upon their own experience.

Balanced and level-headed, William Burdine succeeded in business because he perfected the art of building relationships with his customers over time by giving them a fair deal. He saw being in business as "something for you" (the customer) and "something for me" (the shopkeeper), not as "winner-take-all" for himself.

Burdine was not out for a quick buck or a one-time sale. He believed that he would make a healthy profit, over time, if he simply gave people value at a price they could afford. The rest would take care of itself, he believed, for his customers would be back again and again.

The final words of Burdines' first advertisement in Miami promise its customers "honorable, upright dealing, to merit a share of your patronage, as well as your good will." And that was not just advertising hype. In Mississippi, Central Florida, or South Florida, the name Burdine always was synonymous with the highest standards of business practice. They gave the highest quality of service and merchandise to their customers and perfected the "art of the fair deal."

For William Burdine, it really could not have been any other way. After all, he always had lived in small towns. Verona and Tupelo (Mississippi) and Homeland and Bartow (Florida) were mere specks of places. Miami had a resident population of somewhere between seven hundred and one thousand when he arrived. And no one who is unethical or who does not give customers value can survive in business for long in a place where everybody knows everybody else and word of a raw deal travels fast. In addition, small towns are unforgiving: reputations once sullied can almost never be restored.

No matter where he was, William Burdine never compromised the values that had been instilled in him — nor did he allow others to do so. He never stooped to conquer and never greedily pursued profit at the expense of satisfying his customers.

Principle 2
Short-change Yourself Before You'd Cheat a Customer

Applying this Principle to My Business Success

You Can't Go Wrong By Doing It Right

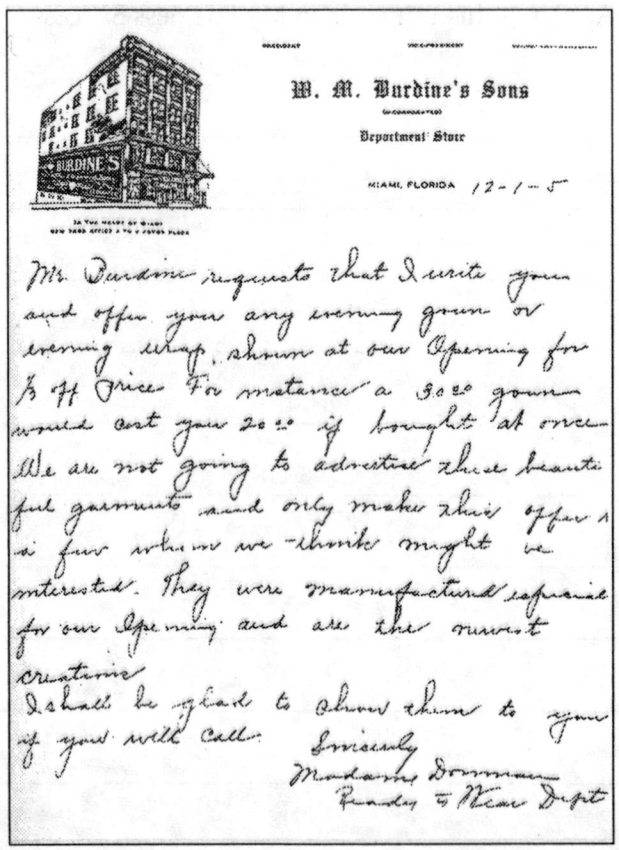

Burdines Archives

This handwritten note apparently dates from 1912. Madame Donnan of the Ready-to-Wear Department wrote to one of her customers, recalling a time when personal service was the order of the day: "Mr. Burdine requests that I write you and offer you any evening gown or evening wrap shown at our Opening for 1/3 off price. For instance a 30.00 gown would cost you 20.00 if bought at once. We are not going to advertise these beautiful garments and only make this offer to a few whom we think might be interested. They were manufactured especially for our Opening and are the newest creations. I shall be glad to show them to you if you will call. Sincerely..."

❖ Success Principle 3

Serve 'Til You Drop

"Ich dien" may be the motto of the Prince of Wales, but it was Burdines who really served. Anyone who has ever looked in vain for a salesperson or who has been ignored or insulted by one (probably every living being on the planet) would have loved shopping at Burdines, for its salespeople were trained to stop just shy of genuflecting before every customer. They radiated a genuine concern and attentiveness for people and actually went out of their way to assist shoppers.

Of course, when an entire business revolves around providing service, each day provides countless examples of how salespeople earn the loyalty of patrons — from the open, friendly, and helpful way in which they greet customers to the precision with which they wrap packages. Most of the time, however, the out-of-the-ordinary, personal gestures are most remembered — sewing a button back onto a patron's dress, even if it wasn't bought at Burdines, at no charge or diverting a child's attention with a lollipop.

Burdines also had no end of regular services to assist its customers. "Jane Grey" telephone and shopping service began as early as in 1920. Never ones to nickel and dime customers, Burdines' stores provided free mail and truck delivery to all customers. In 1947, a temporary parcel post station was opened on the ground floor of Burdines to save Christmas shoppers a trip to the post office.

When Burdines opened its store in West Palm Beach, the

local newspaper ran the headline, "Underlying Principle of New, Expanded Store Is Service." In fact, that statement could have been applied to the opening and running of every Burdines' branch. The reporter observed that "the management endeavors to employ those men and women who almost automatically think in terms of service and public desires" and emphasizes "basic courtesy." And what was service? "To do and say the kindest thing in the kindest way."

The store manager was quoted as saying that "there are people who think of a beautiful store only as a monument to the aggressive enterprise of some towering tycoon," but "we in Burdines are an extremely human lot of Florida folks. We are fortunate in knowing the people in our broad shopping area as good friends and good neighbors. As such we sense their needs and necessities and automatically give them abundantly of that one intangible which they, and we, prize so high: Service. And with a sincere smile."

Principle 3
Serve 'Til You Drop

Applying this Principle to My Business Success

Burdines Archives

As this 1926 photograph shows, Burdines' employees were groomed professionals who knew that there was more to making a sale than just making a sale. They had to be masters of diplomacy, not just knowledgeable about the resiliency of fabrics and the angle of a shirt collar. Sometimes, with a straight face and consummate tact, they even had to take some outrageous piece of merchandise back (losing the battle) in order to keep a customer returning to the store (winning the war).

❖ Success Principle 4

Take It Back. No Questions Asked

About the only thing that you could not return at Burdines was a haircut from one of its beauty salons — but not because Burdines didn't want to. If they could have found a way to make hair grow instantly, they would have done so and joyfully. Burdines' "We'll Take Anything Back, No Matter What, No Matter When" policy was legendary. Everyone has observed or heard of an outrageous example of items being returned and graciously accepted, without a salesperson's missing a beat.

Zada Phipps, Roddey Burdine's daughter, recalls being in the West Palm Beach store when a man asked if he could return a pair of shoes that had been worn for so long they even had holes in them. "Why, of course," said the salesman with a smile and without missing a beat.

A woman once brought back a Chinese-style, primitive, bronze container that she had received as a housewarming gift. "I'd like to return this. It was a present," she said. Failing to find an inventory number after thoroughly examining the item, the saleslady excused herself for a moment. Returning twenty minutes later, she apologized for the delay as she asked the customer to fill in the return merchandise form. "Was there a problem?" the patron asked. "Oh, no," she replied. "It's just that we haven't carried these for three years, so I had to do some checking on the price with another store." The embarrassed customer assured her that this was a gift she had just received. "There is no problem at all," the Burdines' employee answered her. "Don't give it a second thought."

From a sheer dollars-and-cents point-of-view, Burdines believed that the most important thing was never to alienate a customer. Losing a few dollars on the return of a piece of merchandise was nothing compared with how much business could be lost from just one angry customer who decides never to shop at Burdines again or how much negative "press" could be generated by a disgruntled patron. But the key to it all was graciousness. Taking something back bitterly or begrudgingly defeated the purpose of the whole exercise. Salespeople never belittled customers and never looked askance, even if it was obvious that someone was trying to pull a fast one. Burdines always took the high road and treated people with dignity.

Principle 4
Take It Back. No Questions Asked

Applying this Principle to My Business Success

Romer Collection, Miami-Dade Public Library

"Look into the camera, and say 50% off." A motley of Burdines' ordinarily sedate employees dressed as hobos, ragamuffins, and urchins seems to have provided an evening's entertainment for their colleagues.

Burdines went to great lengths to maintain employee morale and a spirit of family. Employees wrote and produced their own publications, which were not subject to managerial approval. And they obviously knew how to let their hair down and put on a good show.

❖ Success Principle 5

Treat Your Employees Like Customers

Founded long before the Age of Throw-away Employees, Burdines generated its bottom line through civility and the mutual respect of management and its employees. Their motto was: "A store is no better than the people who work in it." They believed that any retail business that abused its employees would pay for it at the cash register. They knew that satisfied salespeople make satisfied customers who make substantial purchases and keep coming back to buy even more. They expected professionalism from their employees and treated them with dignity. They recruited good help and set out to keep them for many years because it reduced turnover and saved them money in the long run. So, with those thoughts in mind, they actively cultivated their workforce.

Without coddling or patronizing them, Burdines tried to earn the loyalty of its employees. In 1919, it became "the first store in South Florida to incorporate a well organized program for employee welfare." Organized by Roddey Burdine, what became the Seniority Club was made up of employees with five or more years of service. For workers at those levels, there was the prestige of being invited to semi-annual dinners, a business meeting, and other functions — all at the company's expense. Anyone who was with Burdines for twenty-five years received a $1,000 savings bond. In one newspaper advertisement, Burdines boasted that 55% of its year-round employees had been with the store for five or more years.

At one time, Mrs. Annie Bravo served as Burdines' "Store Mother," looking after the health and general welfare of the female employees. Mrs. Bravo actually would send home employees who appeared too ill to work and she would go so far as to help them "solve the problems of their every day life." At other times, there was a doctor on duty in the store, five days a week, from 2 to 5 p.m., for consultation and simple treatments. There also were three registered nurses on duty continuously. One nurse was even assigned to visit ill employees in their homes.

Due to a housing shortage in Miami that made it more difficult to staff its store, Burdines built four new apartment buildings that were rented to their employees. In 1947, the downtown Miami Burdines was equipped with a special employee lounge and cafeteria, as well as with a solarium on the roof where they could relax, an employee library, hospital, and recreation and quiet rooms.

All Burdine employees knew that, in the eyes of the owners and managers, they were no less important than the customers they served.

Principle 5
Treat Your Employees Like Customers

Applying this Principle to My Business Success

Historical Museum of Southern Florida

When the 1926 hurricane devastated Miami, Roddey Burdine was there to set an example of what one commited man can do to help an entire community. The word philanthropy sounds too formal, even impersonal, for what he did, and charity sounds too condescending. In his understated way, he probably would have said that he just pitched in to do his fair share.

❖ Success Principle 6

Give Where You Live

At least since the nineteenth century, when Tocqueville observed that Americans are consumed by a love of money, this has become a nation of visible, almost compulsive philanthropists, perhaps out of a sense of shame or guilt at having been caught at their venal worst by a foreigner from France.

In truth, smart businesses have long recognized that the buying public adores corporations that give generously from the coffers of their profits and usually rewards them with patronage that increases those profits even more.

Along with catering to its customers and its employees, Burdines valued the larger, growing community around it. When William Burdine brought his family from central Florida south to Miami, the bottom tip of his adoptive state literally resembled an underdeveloped country. He knew that he would have to play a major role in its expansion and full development, for he was wise enough to realize that if the city and the region did not thrive, his store would not either.

Even though they visibly supported the community, the Burdines preferred to do things quietly, behind the scenes, without fanfare. When circumstances called for someone's assuming a leadership role, they did not hesitate to come forward, but they also did not draw attention to themselves.

For example, after the devastating 1926 hurricane, Roddey Burdine personally helped his employees through the disaster, loaning money when it was needed, searching for victims who were not accounted for, and providing shelter for those left homeless. In addition, he even opened his store's warehouses and literally clothed the residents of Miami, giving away fifty thousand garments free-of-charge to hurricane victims who were in need. Roddey, who had become a national figure in retail by 1926, did not hesitate to use his connections outside of Florida to help survivors of the storm. He specifically asked *Women's Wear* to publish a request for anyone to send clothing to Miamians who had lost everything.

Principle 6
Give Where You Live

Applying this Principle to My Business Success

_____

_____

_____

_____

_____

_____

_____

_____

_____

_____

_____

_____

_____

Historical Museum of Southern Florida

Always involving the community, in 1936, Burdines turned the opening of its newest store on Lincoln Road into a festive social occasion. While the musicians took a brief break, Miamians heard a company spokesman reaffirm its commitment to the city and to bringing the best merchandise and latest styles to South Florida.

❖ Success Principle 7

Involve Your Community

Masters of relationship marketing, Burdines could be as subtle as the spider is to the fly, weaving a complex web of entanglements that would make people think of their stores as the center of their civic and social life, "the places to be," well beyond just places of business.

Typically, Burdines would set out to build a committed customer base even before it opened a new store by seeking marketing advice, though they didn't call it that, from leading women in the community, who naturally would be more inclined to patronize and speak well of a store which they had had a hand in helping develop.

Through one clever and generous maneuver, the store would make contributions to the charities of volunteers who would "work" in a given store, for example, by providing shopping services to other customers. A dollar amount equal to the salaries that they would have earned had they been paid employees would be donated by Burdines to their club's charities.

Cultivating customers when they were young, Burdines involved high school students on their "High School Board." These young men and women participated in jamborees and fashion shows and served as hosts and hostesses in the high school shop, subsequently often becoming customers for life.

Some stores were equipped with auditoriums so that clubs and organizations actually could meet on their premises. Opened in largely undeveloped small towns, Burdines really turned its stores into town centers, in which people of all ages could come together for community purposes. Naturally, time and again, the by-product would be long-lasting public relations and tangible sales.

**Principle 7
Involve Your Community**

Applying this Principle to My Business Success

Historical Museum of Southern Florida

"First in Fashion and First in Flight": Looking a little weary but none the worse for wear, two aviators made fashion and airmail history in 1928. Never to be upstaged or bested, Burdines prided itself on setting the pace and leading the pack — in this instance, using the miracle of heavier-than-air-flight and the public's fascination with it to stage the first "Airplane Sale of Dresses," celebrating the first airmail flight from New York to Miami and positioning Burdines as a pacesetter in style.

❖ Success Principle 8

Always Be First — And Always Brag About It

Striving to be first is part of being American and part of being Burdines. People shopped there because it was known as a leader in fashion, in service, in virtually everything that it offered. The fledgling business in a sub-tropical backwater took every opportunity to show that it had come into its own.

Of course, being first only counts if other people learn about it. So, Burdines pulled out the stops, knowing that newspapers love to cover one-of-a-kind or first-ever events and that the public adores pacesetters. Each of the store's many milestones was heralded by unlimited fanfare, celebrating its preeminence and hectoring the competition.

In 1912, Roddey Burdine built and moved his "Winning Store" into its much publicized new headquarters on Flagler Street, the first "skyscraper" in Miami. A five-story building, it was the city's first department store. Burdines boasted the city's first elevator in a retail establishment, as well as its first escalator.

In 1928, Burdines staged the first "Airplane Sale of Dresses," celebrating the first airmail flight from New York to Miami by Pitcairn Airways, predecessor of Eastern Airlines. Thirty-five new evening gowns were flown to Miami from their designers in New York, showing that

Burdines was a mere sixteen hours away from haute couture and clearly first in fashion in the southeast.

With each of Burdines' "firsts" well documented, the buying public could reach for itself the conclusion that it could make things happen faster than any other business in Miami and that, as long as Burdines was around, South Floridians never had to settle for anything like second best — unless they shopped at its competition, of course.

Principle 8
Always Be First — And Always Brag About It

Applying this Principle to My Business Success

Historical Museum of Southern Florida

In 1950, Burdines made headlines when it treated Miami to the "Greatest Christmas Show on Earth," the world's largest Santa Claus. The seven-story lighted Old Nick straddled the bridge connecting the two sections of its downtown Miami store, a holiday tradition that lasted for ten years.

❖ Success Principle 9

Star in Your Own Show

Nothing sells itself. Everything has to be sold, and people have to be attracted into buying. Before the age of television, retail was a major form of public entertainment and the creative energy needed to capture the public's imagination was at a premium. Like P. T. Barnum, though with none of his contempt for patrons, the Burdines were unashamedly showmen. They believed that retail had to be marketed as spectacle. So, if it took having an elephant in the store to bring people in, they brought in an elephant — with good taste, of course.

If putting the largest Santa Claus in the world in lights on the bridge between the two buildings of the downtown Miami store would attract attention, they did so. A crowd of more than 10,000 gathered by mid-afternoon on Thanksgiving night to sing Christmas carols, to see the seven-story lighted Santa, and to shop the next day, on the busiest day of the year — at Burdines, of course.

In 1943, during the Second World War, Burdines hosted an Army Air Forces exhibit to showcase equipment ranging from machine guns to 4,000 pound blockbusters, just one of many sideshows to amuse, enlighten, and divert shoppers.

On a regular basis, people came out in droves to see Burdines' exhibits, lectures, programs for community leaders, special events, fashion shows, and every other manner of spectacle to lure patrons into the store — and keep them there. In fact, special events became a Burdines' trademark.

They were soft-sell opportunities and were used as an early form of subliminal advertising.

In subtle ways, special events reinforced the idea that the store was more than just a store: it was a "living museum," a place in which its customers should feel at home and to which they could come not only to buy, but to learn and experience things that were useful and interesting.

Principle 9
Star in Your Own Show

Applying this Principle to My Business Success

38   You Can't Go Wrong By Doing It Right

Burdines Archives

The title of this 1928 photograph, which appears to have been run in a Burdines' ad, is "Muffin Girl" Now Has a "Muffin Man." Sue Catherine Hall, "the little muffin girl" at the store's tea-roof, is congratulated on her (apparently recent) marriage. Doing business doesn't get more familial than that.

❖ Success Principle 10

Make Your Family Your Business and Your Business Your Family

People worked at Burdines and kept coming back to shop there year after year because they felt it was their family. A family business, Burdines made everyone feel they belonged there. This attitude grew naturally out of William Burdine's small-town upbringing. All his life he not only knew the first name of everyone in town, he could recite their life history and the life story of every member of their family. So, it was automatic that in his trading post, W. M. was known for greeting each of his customers at the door. Nell Coates, who went to work at Burdines in 1926, actually remembered "going to Burdines to buy materials for school clothes and watching the Indian women buying cotton of many colors for their dresses and men's shirts. Burdines was small then, and the owner, Mr. William Burdine...often waited on the customers himself. He was a very pleasant man and knew all his customers by name. When I was only six or eight he would call me by name."

And even after the size of the business increased dramatically, Roddey Burdine prided himself on knowing every employee by name. He was confident that such closeness would rub off on customers and they would never think of shopping anywhere else. R. B. once observed that, like a family, over the years Burdines' employees and patrons together had experienced joyous and sad times —

weddings and births, anniversaries and deaths, as well as every other kind of occasion and circumstance imaginable.

The feeling of family long outlived William and Roddey Burdine. In 1980, on the day that Burdines in downtown Fort Lauderdale was closed and moved to a new location, Jan Gallaher, an employee who first came to work when Harry Truman was president, visited the store on her day off just to be there when they put out the lights for the last time. "At one time," she reminisced, "we knew all the families that came here to shop. We knew the names of the children. We knew which one had the measles, which one had a broken leg and what grades they were in." On that same day, Virginia Hutchinson sat in the cafeteria thinking about a dress that she had bought years before for $15.95. She and scores of "oldtime customers and employees… talked about across-the-counter friendships that began thirty years ago over a stick of lipstick. They remembered Saturday mornings when their mothers took them to Burdines for a new dress and doing the same with their daughters two decades later."

For Peggy McCall, Burdines was a "memory maker." She bought her first knotted string of cultured pearls from the store. She remembers the allure of the cosmetic counters for her and her high school friends. And of course, she recalls rewarding her daughter Carol with a "Snow Princess" and her boys with the "Clown" in the tea room. Long grown, even now the children still remember those treats.

Principle 10
Make Your Family Your Business and
Your Business Your Family

Applying this Principle to My Business Success

42   *You Can't Go Wrong By Doing It Right*

Burdines Archives

This Burdines' window entices shoppers to buy its "Moon Over Miami" fabric and creations, unabashedly capitalizing on the wildly successful song of 1936. The store never missed an opportunity to enhance the effectiveness of its marketing and advertising by using the latest fad, trend, association, or reference in popular culture to its advantage.

❖ Success Principle 11

Keep Your Balance But Ride Every Wave

"If I know one thing about advertising it is that you cannot advertise most effectively in a vacuum," Roddey Burdine might have been heard to say from time to time. "Relate our store promotions to the exciting things going on in the world today."

In the age before television and the power of mass visual media, Burdines had to learn how to multiply the effectiveness of its advertising and marketing by taking advantage of new ideas, fads, or trends in popular culture that swept the country.

In 1936, the song "Moon Over Miami" was the rage, an opportunity made in heaven for a savvy retailer, so Burdines developed its own "Moon Over Miami" fabrics and produced them in anything and everything that people of either sex and any age could wear — handbags, culottes, dresses, blouses, scarfs, belts, hats, teen-age dresses, as well as men's and boy's ties.

Heavier-than-air-flight, the major popular technological wonder of the early decades of the twentieth century, became another popular theme of Burdines' promotions.

After all, a whole world of commercial aviation was opening up and mystifying average men and women.

Effective saleswindows did not statically display merchandise: They had to have strong themes that were attention-getting enough to stop shoppers in their tracks, and they had to sell by sending a clear message or telling a story and using familiar references.

Principle 11
Keep Your Balance But Ride Every Wave

Applying this Principle to My Business Success

---

46   *You Can't Go Wrong By Doing It Right*

Historical Museum of Southern Florida

"Lights, Camera, Action": Burdines single-handedly demonstrated the power of local positioning. It claimed its true place in the spotlight when it developed its most successful marketing sobriquet, "Sunshine Fashions," during the years when Roddey Burdine was president.

❖ Success Principle 12

Cultivate Your Local Garden

Once Burdines had the guts to claim its own identity on its home turf, it boomed. It learned not try to be all things to all people. It discovered the obvious — that its true marketing niche was establishing itself as the store of South Florida, by South Floridians, for South Florida.

Respectably but blandly, for years, the store had been called just W. M. Burdine and Son — and then was known as W. M. Burdine's Sons once the founder died. For a time, it was even known as the somewhat boastful "Winning Store." But during the years when Roddey Burdine matured as president, it found its killer marketing hook.

Using the cheerful phrase "Sunshine Fashions," Burdines did far more than just boast that it was a Florida store. It suggested that the business had come of age, that it knew what its market was. "Sunshine Fashions" implied that Burdines was actually the source of distinctive style for the sub-tropics, that it had cut loose from any outside influences, and that it was for the first time setting the pace in fashion. Eventually, everything from store interiors to clothing styles reinforced and heralded its tropical look.

As a result of "being local," Burdines also set its marketing and merchandise apart from the Miami outlets of northern stores that simply sold last summer's merchandise in the (then thought-to-be) unsophisticated backwater market of South Florida. And in the final twist of irony, "local" went "national," for, eventually, Burdines became a testing ground for styles that would sell around the country and an exporter of summer fashions nationwide — after they had sold in Miami.

In perhaps the ultimate expression of localmania, for one group of visiting northern merchandisers eating in its Tea Room, the store even served a "Florida" luncheon. "Every item was a Florida product or composed of Florida products, from the 'Biscayne vichysoisse' to fresh strawberries to Key lime cream pie."

Burdines mastered the world by conquering its home turf.

Principle 12
Cultivate Your Local Garden

Applying this Principle to My Business Success

Historical Museum of Southern Florida

William Burdine was more than half a century ahead of his time. Some prescient few of his contemporaries may have realized that Miami would develop into a tourist capital. Most who looked at the coastline probably could not see beyond the edge of the shoreline or in front of their noses, however. As early as at the turn of the century, Burdine knew that the economic future of the city and the region lay to the south — even in foreign lands and cultures.

❖ Success Principle 13

Acculturate With Aplomb

The Burdines thought locally, but never parochially. Perhaps, it was a blessing that their store started in backwater Miami. Of necessity, they were forced to look beyond their immediate surroundings and were pressured into thinking and acting globally.

As early as 1903, W. M. Burdine recognized that Miami would be the gateway to the Caribbean and South America and the likely beneficiary of tourism and trade from those regions. Like his father, Roddey Burdine saw the potential in international markets. So, early on, Burdines aggressively marketed its stores in Central and South America. To mark its 58th anniversary in 1956, Burdines sent out 20,000 promotional pieces and invitations to its celebration in Spanish to people throughout Latin America. Then executive vice-president Horace F. Cordes described the effort as pioneering and benefiting more than just Burdines, something "which will help strengthen social and economic ties between Miami and our neighbors to the south."

But beyond just promoting its store to people in other lands, Burdines also took the most crucial (and often neglected) step when it acculturated its store environment. Multi-lingual salespeople were hired to converse in the stores with non-English-speaking customers from around the world, to handle their phone and mail orders, as well as to help foreigners understand differences in the way that business was conducted in the United States. For example, it was especially important to explain that customers in American department stores did not bargain.

Any business can "think globally" — or any other way, for that matter. What counts is taking meaningful action. Burdines knew that any successful international strategy would have to involve its meeting its patrons from other lands more than half way.

Principle 13
Acculturate With Aplomb

Applying this Principle to My Business Success

Romer Collection, Miami-Dade Public Library

Even in black and white, this 1939 picture of one of Burdines' men's furnishings departments feels open, light, and breezy. The store's sub-tropical environments evolved after Roddey Burdine discovered "the power of color." Awash in the pale pastels of Miami's unique palette, the two-story space is free of almost all columns. Indirect lighting, which was essential to creating the sunshine effect, had replaced limited globes of hanging lights by 1938.

❖ Success Principle 14

Grab Your Colors

When Roddey Burdine said to himself, "Eureka, it's our colors!" the normally unexcitable businessman knew that he had found the key to successful retailing and had learned one of the most important lessons of his life — that most of the solutions he sought literally were staring him in the face. From then on, he saw to it that the unique Florida pastel palette transformed his stores into soft reflections of the sub-tropics. Carefully chosen tropical shades distinguished Burdines' fashions and interiors. The stores no longer looked as though they just happened to be located in Florida; they became Florida, inextricably part of the landscape.

According to Dr. Paul George, even the distinctive color, "Biscayne Blue," used by Burdines on its stationary was specially blended to mirror the color of the bay in Miami. R. B. hired noted New York designer Eleanor Le Maire to design the interior of the Miami Beach store because she was said to "design with color and paint with light." She created spacious and calm environments bathed in tropical colors with light woods. In that open, colorful environment, Miss Le Maire set about to "carry out her idea that a modern store must present not merely furniture and merchandise but 'ideas for modern gracious living,' to help the customer picture how these fashions would look and work in their own home." A similar bias to the tropics also was expressed by Raymond Lowey, who decorated the second Burdines on Lincoln Road: "Color styling, lighting, wall decorating and freestanding display have all been keynoted to vacations in the sun."

Customers responded to Roddey's "Eureka" with equally happy exclamations of their own. In the words of Elsie Gordon: "Burdines represented everything that Miami should be — a tropical feeling, colorful resort wear, sea, sun, sand and seashells, and a light and airy decor."

Principle 14
Grab Your Colors

Applying this Principle to My Business Success

_____
_____
_____
_____
_____
_____
_____
_____
_____
_____
_____
_____
_____
_____
_____

Romer Collection, Miami-Dade Public Library

Burdines' store windows had to get potential shoppers to stop, look, and even listen. They had to be clever and attention-getting. Sometimes, they were as subtle as freight trains, even a little corny. Burdines did not hang back, as long as they proved effective.

❖ Success Principle 15

Go for the Gimmick

William Burdine was a master at marketing because his approach was splanchnic, and he did not get bogged down in a lot of folderol. Advertising before the age of radio and television, he had to perfect the art of the gimmick to get customers into his store. From his bag of tricks, he shamelessly promoted the bargain and the freebie, because he studied human nature and what motivates shoppers. A born salesman and promoter, Burdine knew that nothing sells itself; everything has to be sold to someone, so, he always was on the look-out for unusual sales pitches, for ways to appeal to people's instincts, and for opportunities to do the unexpected.

At one time, Burdine offered to pay the round trip or one-way train fare of any potential customer who came to his store from anywhere in Florida — if the person wound up spending certain specified amounts of money.

At another time, Burdines gave shoppers a coupon that was punched to reflect the dollars that they spent throughout the store on a given day. Once their total reached $15.00, they were entitled to a free photograph of themselves, compliments of the photography department.

When W. M. sold his business and his home and furnishings in Mississippi before moving to Florida, he did not advertise in the regular columns of the newspaper, but did the unexpected. He placed short messages throughout the social columns, where they would receive greater attention and have no competition.

If William Burdine were to visit the planet today, he would be stupefied by the advertising pollution in print media, but especially on the airwaves. And he would be aghast at the mixed messages that advertisers send the public. He understood that before he could make a sale, he had to have customers in his store and to achieve that, pure and simple, he needed every gimmick that he (or anyone else) could imagine.

Principle 15
Go for the Gimmick

Applying this Principle to My Business Success

_____
_____
_____
_____
_____
_____
_____
_____
_____
_____
_____
_____
_____
_____
_____

Romer Collection, Miami-Dade Public Library

As this 1948 photograph shows, Burdines' elevator "girls" were outfitted for one week in clothes of 1898 to celebrate the store's 50th anniversary. After that, they wore special uniforms of Burdines' "Anniversary Print" fabrics to keep the festive spirit alive. Burdines always capitalized on the market value of nostalgia.

❖ Success Principle 16

Always Invite Everybody to Your Birthday Party

Burdines loved to celebrate its birthday — and so did its customers, but not just because of birthday sales. The store recognized that nostalgia always is in style and always sells — especially in a region that is young and growing.

In the early years of Miami, while it was a developing community, each year that a store lasted in business was literally a cause for a major celebration for its owners and added to its credibility with the public. So, Burdines went out of its way to generate a mystique surrounding its birthday, even if it was not a milestone.

Of course, at major celebrations, Burdines let out the stops. In 1948, on its 50th anniversary, the store created a print that was made into almost every piece of clothing or accessory that could possibly cover the human body — dresses, blouses, silk scarfs and handbags, berets, bonnets and rollers, little boys' and girls' shirts, men's sport shirts, brunch coats and sundresses with stoles. The print itself was "done in gold, melon or aqua with black outlines of scenes of Burdines' first store, bicycles built for two and nostalgic tracing of yesteryear fashions."

There was a subtle, personal message for Burdines' customers in all of this, too. Because every individual and family celebrates any number of birthdays, anniversaries, and other special occasions during the course of a given year, the store known for going all out to mark its own important days would be positioned in shoppers' minds as the place to shop for their presents as well.

Principle 16
Always Invite Everybody to Your Birthday Party

Applying this Principle to My Business Success

Burdines Archives

Miss Emily Smith came to Miami from England in 1920, when she began working at Burdines. In the company newsletter, she is quoted as saying that she could never work anywhere in America other than at Burdines.

❖ Success Principle 17

Educate Your Customer into Buying

Today, retail has adopted a take-it-or-leave-it attitude: "You like it; buy it. You don't like it; don't buy it. There will be someone else who will. The law of averages is on our side. Eventually, we'll make a sale." Burdines knew that education is the key to all successful sales, and their most successful salespeople spent whatever time it took to work with their customers through to the point of sales.

It was a given that, as professionals, Burdines' employees had to "know" their merchandise inside and out. But the store also sponsored lectures and seminars on a variety of topics that brought consumers into the store and sold merchandise as a by-product.

During the early decades of the twentieth century, Burdines carried a whole range of revolutionary consumer goods and materials now taken for granted, new wonder fabrics among them. So, customers had to be taught about the properties and care of the then new synthetic materials.

In one case, DuPont sent a representative of its textile fibers department to Burdines to speak about "the modern living advantages of women's clothing and home furnishings made of nylon, Dacron polyester fiber, or Orlon acrylic" and about "how the DuPont fibers with their qualities of strength, wrinkle resistance, quick drying, and resistance to moths have sparked a fashion trend to easy-to-care-for clothing."

A key ingredient in the Burdines' brand of sales was the building of trust between salespeople and their clients. Such interactions took considerable time and effort, but, once they were established, a customer could be a customer for life, as many were. Educating store patrons into buying was probably the softest sell there was — and the most effective.

Principle 17
Educate Your Customer into Buying

Applying this Principle to My Business Success

Romer Collection, Miami-Dade Public Library

The men and women who worked at Burdines had to be upbeat and highly presentable. As this 1939 picture shows, Burdines' elevator "girls" had to be the most poised, groomed, and cheerful of all of its employees. The store invested heavily in the image that they conveyed. Their uniforms were designed in different styles for different times of the year, and the colors were changed as often as every three days.

❖ Success Principle 18

Sparkle on the Job

"Look for it over there. If it isn't on the shelf, we don't have it" is the answer customers too often hear today when they ask for sales assistance. In most stores, it is even hard to find someone to ring up a sale. All the jargon of total quality management, Japanese principles of service, and other would-be transformations of retail that companies have flirted with rarely have translated into appreciably better service at the point of purchase.

For Burdines, "the art of doing business" began and ended with the attitude and demeanor of its employees, for no matter what stock was on the shelves, they could not make a sale without a highly presentable and agreeable salesperson. Standing at their elevators with a smile on their face, neatly dressed, and alert, Burdines' elevator "girls" epitomized the image that the store wanted to project through its employees. Because they had contact with so many customers and their image was so important, they spent three of their eight hours on the job actually resting, being coiffed and groomed in the beauty salon, or being fitted for special dresses.

Before anything else, all Burdines' employees were ladies and gentlemen, groomed, not just trained, to do their job. They made eye contact with customers and greeted them with a smile. They took the initiative to offer their services, provide information, and otherwise help people in the store — even passersby who might not be shopping in their department.

Burdines' atmosphere was Southern and Victorian. It was congenial but reserved. Clear standards of social etiquette, which everyone knew, determined behavior. In the atmosphere of studied familiarity, no one would think of calling a customer by his or her first name without permission, as is so often the case today. Above all, it was assumed that people, no matter what their rank as employees, would respect each other's privacy.

It is easy to be well groomed on the outside, but it is impossible to camouflage a mean spirit or disgruntled nature within. Anyone who worked at Burdines knew that a genuine joyfulness and enthusiasm were prerequisites for their job — and for their staying with the company.

Principle 18
Sparkle on the Job

Applying this Principle to My Business Success

Historical Museum of Southern Florida

Miami, 1898

Miami's tent city bivouacing American troops waiting to invade Cuba still might have been one of the first sights that greeted William Burdine and his family when they arrived in 1898 — even though the troops were leaving, because the ten-week Spanish-American war was over. The presence of 7,000 soldiers in need of supplies is what attracted W. M. and a generation of pioneers from Central and North Florida to the city.

Conditions obviously were primitive, and the men were restive in the summer heat of South Florida with little or no meaningful diversions — especially when it became clear that they would not be invading Cuba and, in fact, that the war would soon be over.

❖ Success Principle 19

Expand — Even in Bad Times

The late nineteenth and early twentieth centuries were times of rapid expansion in South Florida, but the relentless boom and bust of the Miami economy could unsettle even the most savvy businessman. As populations grew and the landscape was transformed into a tourist paradise, only those businesses that knew how to expand, no matter what the financial climate, survived the competition. Of course, anybody could run a profitable business when the economy was strong. The trick was to come out of the bad times positioned to capture the market on the upswing.

At first, in 1898, William Burdine looked upon his opening a trading post in Miami as a way of offsetting a slowdown in business at his store in Bartow. Eventually, he chose not only to come to Miami but to close his Central Florida store, even after he learned that most of the seven thousand troops would soon be leaving the area as the Spanish-American War fizzled out.

In 1936, after the devastations of a serious hurricane and national depression, Roddey Burdine boldly opened a branch on Lincoln Road in Miami. And even during the depression itself, Roddey added a wing to the new Sears, from which he operated a short-lived resort shop. On a much broader scale, Roddey pictured Burdines eventually with branches everywhere in Florida.

The key to the Burdines' strategy was to protect their existing customer base and to increase their market share — to dominate, if not to monopolize retail. In a growing environment, they knew that there always would be customers, even if they had to wait for the population to catch up to them. Most important of all, they were willing to re-invest their profits for long-term growth rather than to take their short-term gains out of the business.

Principle 19
Expand — Even in Bad Times

Applying this Principle to My Business Success

Burdine Archives

What better device than putting its models and its fashions in an expensive "Flying Cloud" Reo against the backdrop of the exclusive Miami Biltmore and the Venetian Pools to prove that Burdines had gone chic and could claim to have developed its own style? The headline for the 1928 ad in which this photograph appeared proclaims that "Four Fashionables Go A-motoring." Without a doubt, under Roddey Burdine's leadership, the store's image had progressed well beyond its trading post days.

❖ Success Principle 20

Develop a Hallmark Style

"We always need to be different. If our customers can buy something anywhere, why should they buy it from us?" Roddey Burdine might have said. "Same old, same old doesn't sell. Our unique fashion makes our business and, indirectly, it sells everything in the store."

R. B. knew that the truly distinctive fashions a store carries typically become a walking promotion for all of its inventory — from household goods to accessories. The unique, stylish, and attention-getting clothes that patrons wear can turn them into moving billboards for a store, setting in motion the most powerful advertising of all — word-of-mouth. "Where did you buy that beautiful dress?" "At Burdines, of course!"

According to *Miami Herald* fashion editor Marilyn Clark, "Burdines always made itself felt as a strong fashion leader." Even when it opened as little more than a trading post, it stanced itself as an authority on style. In the 1890's, it set out to sell women on using hand-held fans for their comfort in the sub-tropics and "cautioned them to select smaller, headhugging hats."

"Fashion shows began as early as 1914, when the store held concerts, and society ladies of the day modeled the latest fashions, influenced at that time by the outbreak of World War One. New-found freedoms were expressed in straight shifts worn with a belt at the hips, compressed bodies in tube shapes denied all trace of femininity and cloche hats that concealed boyish hair were the style."

Ever the pacesetter, in 1928, Burdines presented a "Revue of Fashion," after its buyers made their first trips to Europe. Begun in 1929, many of the "Sunshine Fashions" that Burdines developed specially for each winter season in Florida became "fashions for the nation as a whole the following summer."

Because of its distinctive styles, Burdines became nationally known to others in the retail industry and to the general consumer, many of whom would make a point of visiting its store during the winter in Miami. "You see," Roddey Burdine might have said with a smile, "because we strive truly to be different, people beat a path to our doors."

Principle 20
Develop a Hallmark Style

Applying this Principle to My Business Success

Historical Museum of Southern Florida

Burdines planted itself on what eventually became Flagler Street in 1900 — and has never left. A man who rolled with the punches a good deal of his life, William Burdine also might have philosophized that eventually the world comes to you if you stay in the same place long enough — especially if you are wise enough to recognize where the downtown business district of a growing city may be.

❖ Success Principle 21

Always Use One Hand To Wash the Other

In every situation, there are would-be leaders and real leaders. By all accounts, Burdines was in a class by itself, behaving even like a corporate savior. It put the needs of Miami and its citizens first and foremost on its agenda, exhibiting the kind of leadership that people never forget.

Burdines built a successful image by never deviating from its support of its local community. It knew that if the Miami economy was thriving, it too would prosper. But no policy endeared the store more to Miami than its 1945 policy of supporting the local economy by buying everything that it possibly could, from sportswear and handbags to confections, from vendors in the city, because that kind of loyalty translated into jobs for South Floridians.

According to store regulations, Burdines' divisional managers were instructed to "find out what Miami manufacturers have to offer before sending buyers anywhere else."

On October 31, 1945, *The Miami Herald* reported that on behalf of sixty manufacturers, Arthur Kahn, president of the Miami Fashion Council, publicly stated that "Burdines had contributed more to the success of Miami manufacturing than any other individual store or group."

Once again, Burdines proved that to be a success in business, you sometimes have to give before you can get.

Principle 21
Always Use One Hand To Wash the Other

Applying this Principle to My Business Success

Melissa Curry

Burdines associated itself with premier activities in South Florida as a way of gaining recognition without blowing its own horn. Master of the subtle promotional pitch, Roddey Burdine knew how to turn celebrity, sports, and being in Miami to his company's advantage. One of the area's best amateur golfers and president of the Miami Country Club for many years, he promoted the city as a sports capital by attracting leading players and other notables to participate in tournaments. Of course, Burdines benefited from having its name associated with events that routinely generated positive publicity. In this picture, R.B. was part of a foursome that included Ben Hogan, Babe Ruth, and John Evans Junkin.

❖ Success Principle 22

Don't Shout, But Always Get Your Name Out

Some promoters think that the only kind of advertising worth doing is the sort that makes the cash register ring right now, today — for a January White sale or the Fourth of July — and that nothing else matters. Such promotions are the only ones that are measurable, they argue. You advertise an item, people come into the store (or they don't), and you tally the sales. If the ratio between the dollars spent and the revenue generated is acceptable, your advertising is a success. End of story. If you are going to spend money hawking something, you better be able to prove that the dollars provoked enough business to more than pay for itself, without delay — or else.

In fact, as promotional sophisticates are well aware, there are ways to sell without overtly appearing to do so. Without abandoning direct purchase promotions, Burdines perfected the kind of subtle conditioning of the public mind that would later be known as institutional advertising, the purpose of which was to put its name "in the air" and to make and keep it a household word.

For one thing, the store sponsored its own radio program, hosted by "Enid Bur," whose name was an anagrammatic play on its own. To the strains of "Beyond the Blue Horizon," a fitting melody for the Miami sub-tropics, Ms. Bur managed to hold forth with fashion news, household hints, interviews, recordings — and even a shopping guide to Burdines, the whole less than subliminal point of the show, of course.

In addition, Roddy Burdine helped organize and promote big golf tournaments in the late 1920's and early 30's, bringing the sport's best known celebrities to Miami — and positioned his name and the store's with quality, high profile activities that benefited everybody.

Of course, the lesson in all this may be hard to learn in today's age of media one-upmanship: with rare exceptions, less is more and strategic positioning, more than promotional blather, is everything. Sometimes a quiet and persistent sales message rings truest and most effectively over time.

Principle 22
Don't Shout, But Always Get Your Name Out

Applying this Principle to My Business Success

Historical Museum of Southern Florida

Eventually, they came by land, by sea, and by air — tourists, the lifeblood of Miami. Burdines encouraged them to travel light. The less they brought with them, the more they would have to buy.

❖ Success Principle 23

If You Want To Be a Big Fish, You Can't Swim in a Small Pond

Some whiz kid at Burdines may have surprised his senior colleagues and himself when he just blurted out, "It's almost too late to reach tourists once they are here. We should advertise nationally." Or the genius who came up with the store's slogan, "Bring Your Trunks Empty," may have realized that her concept could only make sense if ads were placed outside of Florida.

However the idea of a national advertising strategy came about, it broke new ground not only for Burdines, but for all of retail. According to William Bischoff, "Burdines was the first American department store to recognize the value of advertising outside its own commuting area. It was the first department store to advertise in national magazines and in newspapers a thousand or more miles away from its own doors. New visitors to Miami know about Burdines before they arrive."

National advertising was not just a cute idea whose time had come; it was a matter of corporate survival. Burdines was a big fish in a small pond that was overstocked with tourists during the brief winter season and, as time went on, with increased competition. It had to cast its net wider and wider to ensure that it would keep its share of the market. It would have been easier, less expensive, and lazy of Burdines just to wait for customers to come to Miami, as it and other businesses always had. Instead, it had the foresight to turn its advertising into a preemptive strike, miles ahead of its closest competition, proving once again that every standard operating procedure needs to be questioned and updated.

Principle 23
If You Want To Be a Big Fish, You Can't Swim in a Small Pond

Applying this Principle to My Business Success

_____
_____
_____
_____
_____
_____
_____
_____
_____
_____
_____
_____
_____
_____
_____

94   *You Can't Go Wrong By Doing It Right*

Double-dealers and two-timers don't make it in small towns. Once they are found out, no one will do business with them. W. M. Burdine spent most of his life in Verona, Mississippi, steeped in small-town values. This picture of Main Street, Verona was taken twenty years after the Burdines left for Homeland, Florida, but it is probably close to what the business district looked like when they lived there. In fact, W. M.'s pharmaceutical business actually may have been located on Main Street.

❖ Success Principle 24

Eschew Gobbledygook

No corporation can afford to be so candid and honest that it gives away trade secrets or exposes itself to liability, but it cannot lie to the public or obfuscate matters and get away with it for long. Nor can it refuse to face facts about its corporate strengths and weaknesses without paying a high price. Fortunately for Burdines, it had nothing to hide, so it consistently told the truth and listened to the truth. Its public relations were rather straightforward and uncomplicated.

In 1933 and 1949, it took the offensive. Burdines "went public" to protect its image and to quash what it called "rumors detrimental to our business" from unspecified quarters. In the process, it publicly disclosed the source of its ownership, its mortgage indebtedness, its promptness in paying its bills, and other matters pertaining to its corporate conduct — and revealed the solid picture of its organizational health.

Burdines also expected honesty from its employees in assessing its organizational strengths and weaknesses. By 1947 its progressive executives had conducted the company's fourth "Stech Survey." Through the process, the store boasted, "Every employee of Burdines is urged to express his frank opinion and criticism." The results were "compiled...to serve as a tool for enlightened leadership and improved working conditions. The questionnaires we fill out...are kept as confidential as a diplomat's brief case. Yes, we can all air our private views on how we think a store should be run! We can toss our bouquets and brickbats in any direction and know the questionnaires we've filled out will never be seen by anyone connected with Burdines." After the results of the survey were tabulated by Stech in New York, the final results were submitted to Burdines' management.

Burdines knew that to be believable in the eyes of its customers and the general public, it would have to take the initiative in clarifying matters pertaining to its reputation. It did not cop out by pleading "No comment," nor did it beat around the bush. Instead, it was frank, forthright, and fair in its public pronouncements.

Principle 24
Eschew Gobbledygook

Applying this Principle to My Business Success

_____
_____
_____
_____
_____
_____
_____
_____
_____
_____
_____
_____
_____
_____
_____

Burdines Archives

Go team Burdines. On June 23, 1926, opening night of the Hialeah Fronton, Madison Brumbach (right) and Robert Conroy of the store's Jai-Alai team handily defeated their opponents. In addition to receiving recognition from the league, they earned a cash award from the store. Working at Burdines was a way of life, not just a job. The store was loyal to its employees and was out to build loyalty from them as well.

❖ Success Principle 25

Promote from Within

Burdines' preeminent success came about directly because it was committed to grooming its employees for their own success. "Loyalty," "commitment," "longevity," "career," "seniority," "lifetime," "dedicated" — these are just some of the words used to describe the relationship between employee and employer during the early decades of the store. Proudly, in one newspaper advertisement, the company boasted that of its "fifty-three executive and department managers, forty-six have worked their way up in the store — and tomorrow's top-flight executives are coming up today, by the same route."

Of course, what people then did as employees or employers was very different from what they can do today. In the early decades of the twentieth century, hardly anyone went to work or employed someone for the short haul. Then, many more people looked upon their jobs as careers than do so today. In addition, it ran against every sensibility of the age to treat workers as disposable commodities. Downsizing, as acceptable standard operating procedure to increase corporate profits, was virtually unheard of. And, finally, legal restrictions on employers' hiring, firing, and every other kind of labor practice were virtually non-existent. Almost everywhere, it was an employer's job market.

Still, Burdines wanted to be known as a premier employer. It knew that it would only attract the best help if it had a reputation for dealing fairly with its employees. Practically, it was much cheaper in the long run to keep employees, even when business was slow, than it was to train them and let them go. Its Seniority Club recognized and financially rewarded people who stayed with the company.

More than anything else, promoting from within insured the continuity of Burdines' corporate culture. It was not about to let unknown quantities move it in directions contrary to its long-standing policies and general way of doing business. In an era of delayed gratification, employees expected to learn the ropes, to move up through the ranks, and to earn a fair increase in stature or pay that they achieved through time on the job. They did not expect to become overnight successes.

Principle 25
Promote from Within

Applying this Principle to My Business Success

102   *You Can't Go Wrong By Doing It Right*

Florida State Archives

Over time, Burdines appears to dominate downtown Miami, even as its covered sidewalks and awnings protect it and its patrons from the swelter of the sub-tropical sun.

❖ Success Principle 26

Think Big, But Not Gargantuan

William Murrah Burdine was lucky enough to have been born with cautious genes. The rest of his healthy skepticism for flamboyance he learned during his youth in Mississippi. In his world, people were reserved, thought things through before they ventured into something radically new, and covered their bases. So, when W. M. and his family arrived in South Florida in 1898, they were well fortified against any temptation to succumb to the enticements of get-rich-quick schemes.

Obviously, in a growing region, thinking big almost may be inevitable: It may be nothing more than a matter of keeping up with burgeoning market demand. But it also may be the undoing of anyone who moves too quickly. Luckily for them, the Burdines stayed above the boom-and-bust mentality that has seen fortunes made and lost in Miami.

W. M. and Roddey were successful when other businessmen failed, in part, because they never bet the store and in part because they did not just respond to frenzied growth but had a plan of their own. For one thing, as a general rule, they did not come in hastily at the beginning of a new boom, when it was almost too late to profit from it. Instead, they positioned themselves during a bust, so that they were already in place, anticipating the start of the next upward trend. That was the case in 1925, when Burdines profited from the boom, but Roddey Burdine rightly sensed that a bust was coming, so he did not get caught up in the speculation.

Overall, the Burdines took the time to phase in their expansion to meet what would be real needs and thereby avoided the speculative pitfalls that torpedoed other businesses. Originally attracted to Miami by the prospect of selling to the 7,000 troops in the region, they saw that bubble burst almost immediately when the Spanish-American War came to an end almost before it began, but they did not let that discourage them. They knew that the wiser course was to be ready for the next upswing in business when profits were likely to be even bigger and more solid.

Principle 26
Think Big, But Not Gargantuan

Applying this Principle to My Business Success

_____
_____
_____
_____
_____
_____
_____
_____
_____
_____
_____
_____
_____
_____

106   *You Can't Go Wrong By Doing It Right*

Florida State Archives

Burdines drew crowds into its stores other than for shopping, believing that one good thing would lead to another. This 1928 photograph shows the rooftop restaurant of the downtown Miami Burdines, a popular and fashionable meeting place. A quartet provided live music for patrons. The sweeping view of the city was an added attraction.

❖ Success Principle 27

Magnetize Your Business

Burdines turned itself into one big attraction for customers. Long before anyone ever heard the phrase shopping mall, Burdines was using the concept. Its stores were not conceived of only as places where people shopped but where they congregated.

Knowing that people spend money where they are comfortable, Burdines designed stores that would make people feel relaxed, in "a home away from home" and even in "an office away from the office." It seduced its customers.

In the men's grill, there were round conference tables and plug-in telephones so that businessmen would stay in the store and conduct their deals. Writing desks were provided for busy customers in the Hibiscus lounge of the downtown Miami store. The Book Store and Lending Library was a place where local literary people gathered. The beauty salon held women captive for hours.

Consistent with Burdines' successful marketing strategy, the rooftop restaurant was used as another way to condition men and women to come into the store, even if they were not buying merchandise on a given day, so that when they did eventually think about shopping, they would "naturally" think about going to Burdines.

Principle 27
Magnetize Your Business

Applying this Principle to My Business Success

Historical Museum of Southern Florida

Basking in art deco understatement, a far cry from its original trading post, Burdines' Boulevard Shop exudes the look of quiet elegance that it eventually cultivated.

❖ Success Principle 28

Sell Nothing But The Best

The most overworked and least credible phrase in advertising is "the best." Companies that claim to offer the best products and services to the public or to be committed to doing so appear to be ho-hum.

First of all, too many people have been disappointed by overblown claims. Secondly, even though what is "the best" would appear to be obvious to everyone, upon closer examination, it is really a highly subjective and complex call. "Who are they trying to kid?" almost any savvy consumer would ask. "Surely, their hotshot promotional department could come up with some- thing better than insisting that they are 'the best.'"

Yet, with a certain innocence and bravado, Burdines was so brazen as always to pursue the best in everything it did — and to say that it was doing so. When he was president, Roddey Burdine especially looked at his store as a way of exposing people to the undisputed best things in the world — from designer dresses to linens — that he could have a role in making part of their lives. He did not see himself just as running a business, but as able through that business to raise the quality and enjoyment of life.

And it didn't stop with things. Burdines communicated an intangible feeling of quality about everything it did, even though it sold tangible goods and provided services. The collective impression that it made upon the public was that whatever Burdines did was "the best."

Perhaps what made Burdines different from other stores was that it pursued the best of everything. It did not conduct any part of its business by shortcut. It did not offer the highest quality in one area so that it could scimp in another.

Burdines' mystique has been the direct result of the perception it created that anyone who shopped there would receive the best merchandise, the best price, the best service, the best return policy, the best overall shopping experience — and it was perceived as "the best" by the buying public.

Principle 28
Sell Nothing But The Best

Applying this Principle to My Business Success

Romer Collection, Miami-Dade Public Library

Dignity is rarely the by-product of stiffness or formality. If anything, it comes from the ease of doing the right thing at the right time, without even thinking about it. Burdines created an atmosphere in which people were not afraid to be themselves. Looking as though they worked anywhere but in one of the nation's premier retailers, these Burdines' employees knew how to drop their guard — and recover it at exactly the right time.

❖ Success Principle 29

Humanize Humans

Today, the vast majority of businesses treat people as though they are a disposable commodity. It is all too commonplace to hear about C.E.O.'s who euphemistically downsize hundreds or thousands of employees simply to raise the value of their company's stock and to increase their own compensation package. Quarterly fluctuations in the stock market have become much more important than the long-term contribution of people working on behalf of a corporation.

Similarly, companies have grown contemptuous of the general public. They hold the average consumer at bay by handling their questions and complaints through robotic menus on the telephone. And they have so monopolized markets, that shoppers have little choice but to take what they are given.

By contrast, in an almost spiritual way and as a direct outgrowth of its founder's life, Burdines' world stressed the abiding value of people, no matter who they were. William Burdine's father was a Methodist minister and he grew up in a deeply religious household. Everywhere in the small towns of America in which he lived, he saw that because of people coming together for a common generous purpose houses were built, whole towns were saved from natural disaster, and families were helped out of their personal losses and distress.

Furthermore, it is no accident that a man who was dehumanized as a prisoner of war for six and one half months during the Civil War eventually created a business enterprise that had at its heart the respect of human dignity — beyond the bottom line. William Burdine saw firsthand that even when people had to endure physical deprivation and humiliation, they were able to dig deep into the core of their being and find the strength to survive.

It became axiomatic in William Burdine's thinking that anything that succeeded in business or in life had to be based upon dignifying people. He knew that if he was going to be able to create anything of lasting value, he had to find a way to tap into the indefinable something at the core of every human being that motivates them to think and work beyond themselves and for a larger purpose.

Principle 29
Humanize Humans

Applying this Principle to My Business Success

118   You Can't Go Wrong By Doing It Right

Florida State Archives

Imagine being middle-aged, leaving your home, and setting out to build a new life and fortune — only to have your greatest hopes dashed. The prospect of striking "orange gold" lured William Burdine to Central Florida, but success eluded him. Like the citrus grove shown in this picture, his crop was destroyed by frost in the mid-1890's.

❖ Success Principle 30

Don't Become Attached to Anything

William Burdine's motto should have been "Never Look Back." At eighteen, W. M. left his home to fight in the Civil War, not knowing if he would ever return alive. Taken prisoner of war, he never knew if he would survive the ordeal. He lost his first wife and two of their children. At forty-seven, he sold his business, left his native Mississippi, and moved to Florida. When his citrus groves in Homeland were destroyed, he was resilient enough to go into the retail business. And when that business proved disappointing, at fifty-five, he and his family packed up and moved to Miami.

One experience after another in his life taught W. M. the harshest, but perhaps most useful, survival lesson of all: that to succeed a person has to learn to be detached — to move on, not to live in the past, not to let his emotions cloud his judgment, not to become wedded to doing things a certain way or to expecting things to happen as they always had, and to accept even the most unthinkable and devastating changes in life as givens.

As a result, in business, as in life, Burdine was a pragmatist's pragmatist. He believed that a businessman had to change with the times and be willing to start from scratch — over and over, if necessary. In addition to his broad philosophy, Burdine taught his son Roddey the basics: "If something isn't selling, put it on sale." And he was astute enough to recognize that if an idea wasn't working, it was only good business to rework it or replace it with a viable alternative. "If life has taught me one thing it is that people and businesses survive only if they are flexible," he would have insisted.

**Principle 30
Don't Become Attached to Anything**

Applying this Principle to My Business Success

Historical Museum of Southern Florida

In the 1920's suspended lights with large frosted globes and merchandise in row after row of showcases were considered state-of-the-art design. Within about ten years, however, Burdines would transform its interiors into the open, airy, colorful environment that complemented the niche which it cultivated as the Florida Store and the creator of Sunshine Fashions.

❖ Success Principle 31

Keep Your Overhead Low, and Sell, Sell, Sell

The formula for Burdines' early financial success was its low overhead and high sales volume. They knew instinctively that too many businesses fail under the weight of their own operating costs, not simply because they do not generate sufficient revenues.

So, Burdines stayed managerially lean. In the early years, ninety percent of its employees were on the floor selling. There was little if any administrative overhead, so almost everyone pulled his own weight, and the few who did not do so by generating direct sales could justify their positions as essential for the conduct of business.

Gracious and understated, the Burdines were reserved about everything, except about selling. They never wanted anyone who worked for them to get the idea that they could just sit back and wait for business to happen. In retail as they knew it, if you don't sell, you don't make sales, so you don't have a business. No one had the luxury of enjoying a free ride.

If someone had suggested that they really needed to have a battle cry to egg the salesforce onto the floor, Roddey Burdine would probably have commissioned the writing of something that sounded like the 1812 Overture. A born cheerleader, R. B. relished firing up the troops himself by telling everyone to "sell, sell, sell."

Principle 31
Keep Your Overhead Low, and Sell, Sell, Sell

Applying this Principle to My Business Success

Historical Museum of Southern Florida

To work at Burdines someone had to have been a real salesperson, not just an order-taker. This ad underscores the experience and professionalism of the staffs of their men's clothing and hat departments. In an obvious bid to make tourists feel comfortable dealing with someone from their part of the country or even their hometown, the copy identifies the (in some cases several) states in which the salesmen have lived, the other stores in which they have worked, and the areas in which they specialized. In addition, to help customers know exactly which salesperson to seek out, the entire staff proudly was pictured in the advertisement as well.

❖ Success Principle 32

Don't Train Your Salespeople: Groom Them

Professional salespeople were a key to Burdines' success. When the company was family-owned, there were no self-service departments. Merchandise was not accessible on racks or in piles. Items that were kept on full view were typically arranged in glass cases, so customers could not rummage through inventory at will, as they commonly do today. In the dress department, a customer sat down, told a saleslady what kind of dress she was looking for, and then was personally shown one dress after another until she found one that she liked.

So, salespeople did not just have to be effective; they had to be consummate professionals. They were Burdines' link to every person who walked into the store, a major part of the reason why people made purchases and crucial to its success.

Roddey Burdine boasted that "every department will be under the supervision not of a mere clerk, but of a salesman or saleswoman, each an expert in their line." They had to know their merchandise and really had to know how to sell by working with a customer, suggesting a more flattering style or color, and knowing a client's needs better than he or she actually did.

The key to effective sales is not simply knowing how to close a sale, but how to conduct the full sales process. The best Burdines' salespeople built a relationship with a customer over time. In that way, they knew how to anticipate a client's likes and dislikes before they even said anything.

When something went on sale that they knew would appeal to a certain customer, they would call with the good news that they had found "something that looks as though it was made for you — and it's on sale." Seasoned pros could probably recite the better part of what was in a client's wardrobe and his or her buying history as well.

Burdines trained its salespeople obsessively to follow-up on every sale and to understand that selling to a customer never ends, but continues even after the patron has left the store.

**Principle 32
Don't Train Your Salespeople: Groom Them**

Applying this Principle to My Business Success

130   *You Can't Go Wrong By Doing It Right*

Historical Museum of Southern Florida

When is an escalator more than just a series of moving stairs? When it is turned into a marketing ploy, of course. This 1936 photo of "three women descending" what was then a marvel of applied technology speaks volumes about "thoroughly modern" Burdines, the company that always set out to have the latest in everything.

❖ Success Principle 33

Go for the Gizmos and Gadgets

Almost everybody but the inveterate Henry David Thoreau clones of each generation succumbs to the lure of the bells and whistles of his age.

Burdines was obsessed with being the first kid on the block to have the latest technology, because it was good marketing (something to lord over the competition), it brought people into the store (they came in in droves just to see the marvels for themselves), and because it could help them serve customers more efficiently.

Burdines' five-story "skyscraper" was the first retail business in Miami to have an elevator, complete with an operator, of course. It installed the largest escalator in Florida. (Imagine the attraction for kids trying to go up the wrong way!) In 1951, it was the first to install Otis Automatic elevators operated by electronic touch buttons. (Goodbye elevator girls! Hello stopping at every floor, thanks to those kids again.) And of course, Burdines introduced the only lighted escalator south of Memphis, as soon as it was available.

In later years, the tradition continued. Using the then infant medium of television, to promote a myriad of products throughout the store, Burdines claimed to have "launched the biggest closed circuit color television production in history." Its auditorium was converted into a broadcast studio, from which seventy-five consumer goods were shown on twenty-one-inch monitors at fifty different locations throughout the store. Presumably, no shopper could escape seeing at least something of the marvel. The advertising was offset by newscasts, comedy, and interviews with t.v. personalities and professional talent.

Frank Peterson, Jr., the store vice president in charge of the project, recalls that when noted t.v. star Ed Sullivan appeared in the store on the last day of the spectacle, Burdines was so swamped with people that they could not do any business — a reminder that every solution breeds another set of problems.

Principle 33
Go for the Gizmos and Gadgets

Applying this Principle to My Business Success

Romer Collection, Miami-Dade Public Library

The congested view looking west on Flagler Street in 1939 confirmed William Burdine, Sr.'s sense in 1900 that the street would eventually become Miami's major downtown commercial center. Burdines remains the tallest building on the block. It adopted its distinctive "Sunshine Fashions" slogan in 1929.

❖ Success Principle 34

Leave Whirling to the Dervishes

Today, it is commonplace to say that people who are successful in business have to have a vision of their company's future, and that if they don't, they are unfit to do the job. The problem is that most people wouldn't know a vision if they saw one and confuse megalomania, divination, and hallucination for the real thing.

As both W. M. and R. B. Burdine would have told it, people who build businesses have to keep both feet firmly on the ground, while they are clearly looking ahead. They have to be visionary realists or realistic visionaries, whichever the case may be. For certain, they knew that wishing for success doesn't make it so.

The Burdines were men of vision who saw well beyond the reality that was in front of them, and they would have been the first to say that any successful business is the result of inspired leadership. They were also pragmatic and realistic, grounded in the nuts-and-bolts of developing a business that already was operating. Most often, what looks like having vision, they would have pointed out, really results from combining two already known quantities to make something new, or from seeing something old in a new light. Furthermore, they would have been quick to point out that people who have vision need to be able to act upon their insights; otherwise, there is little point in having them — or certainly little effect.

W. M. realized that Flagler Street would become the business center of downtown Miami long before others did, but only by seeing to it that his business moved there did he make it happen. Had he not done so, perhaps his "vision" might not have been realized.

Roddey Burdine could entertain all sorts of visions for a statewide chain of glamorous stores, but at the same time he reminded himself and his contemporaries that his primary business was in Miami, and that his customer base came from "essentially a sports city, a playground in winter, a home for those who seek quiet and outdoor recreation."

Today, he might have said that he and any successful businessman always needed to do two things at once: stick to his core business and objectively assess its strengths and weaknesses — and, at the same time, keep an open mind to new possibilities.

**Principle 34
Leave Whirling to the Dervishes**

Applying this Principle to My Business Success

_____
_____
_____
_____
_____
_____
_____
_____
_____
_____
_____
_____
_____
_____

Burdines Archives

Looking as uncomfortable as he no doubt was, William Murrah Burdine, Jr. (right) is shown cutting the Burdines' 52nd Anniversary cake, while George Whitten looks on.

A recluse, who preferred fishing in the Everglades and socializing among the Seminoles to presiding in the corporate board room, "Uncle Willie," as members of his family affectionately called him, was the least fitted of all the Burdine sons to head the family business. His brother, Roddey, tried to awaken his interest in retail, but to no avail.

❖ Success Principle 35

Walk the Floor

Today, it is too easy for C.E.O.'s and other business executives to get out of touch with their own companies. "There was a time when I knew the name of every employee, but now we have grown too big for that," too many people sigh with a certain self-satisfaction.

In addition, as their companies grow, senior management tend to restrict their corporate maneuvers to the boardroom, where they can convince their directors to approve such ideas as issuing more stock, fending off a leveraged buy-out, or merging with or acquiring another corporation. Worst of all, they get information about their business secondhand from hired guns and consultants. Yet, as important as those activities and sources of intelligence clearly are, they cannot take the place of a C.E.O.'s knowing what is really going on — firsthand.

As the Burdines could have told them, no one can run a successful business in a cocoon for long. "You must keep your eyes and ears open and get down there on the sales floors so that you can see what is happening, what customers are buying, how they are being treated," Roddey Burdine would have told his managers. "That's how you do a market survey that means anything."

The store president regularly could be seen walking the floor and jotting down notes in his little black book — and he expected others to do the same. Each executive had to spend at least one or two hours in the trenches. After all, that's where the business was.

Walking the floor was not simply a way to look over everybody's shoulder and keep them on their toes, though it did that, of course. It also had the very positive effect of breaking down the barriers between management and employees, as well as between management and customers, and fostering the kind of family atmosphere that was a major reason for Burdines' success.

Principle 35
Walk the Floor

Applying this Principle to My Business Success

142   You Can't Go Wrong By Doing It Right

Historical Museum of Southern Florida

In 1912, Roddey Burdine built and moved Burdines, "The Winning Store," into its much publicized new headquarters on Flagler Street, the first "skyscraper" in Miami. A five-story building boasting the city's first elevator in a retail establishment, the facility at first was too large for Burdines itself, which only occupied the first two floors. The remaining three floors were rented until Burdines eventually expanded into them.

❖ Success Principle 36

Always Spy on Other Businesses

Spying (or its less sinister-sounding synonym, "information gathering") is a necessary part of any business. No one can succeed for long who does not assess external conditions, watch what the competition is doing, and keep up with trends.

Perhaps because Roddey Burdine never went to college and therefore, in his own eyes, lacked certain necessary formal credentials, he had an insatiable appetite for learning everything that he could about retail. He was never content with the status quo, was always on the lookout for new ways of doing and improving business, and never hesitated to imitate something that he thought was promising.

Whenever he traveled, Burdine visited other retail establishments so that he could spot and adopt a new concept, a promising line of merchandise, or the most up-to-date form of customer service or technology.

R. B. was happiest, of course, when he could report that Burdines actually was a leader in the industry. But he would have been the first to say that "we are the leader, because we take nothing for granted and certainly don't rest on our laurels. So we must be ever more vigilant in the future to maintain our number one position."

Principle 36
Always Spy on Other Businesses

Applying this Principle to My Business Success

Historical Museum of Southern Florida

Roddey Burdine's modest and unassuming side was apparent not only in his management style, but also in his public presence. He never sought accolades or recognition. In August 1937, a year and a half after his sudden death, the Miami City Commission unanimously voted to name the city's new municipal stadium "The Roddey Burdine Stadium." Years later, Burdine's name was dropped from the building, and it was renamed "The Orange Bowl."

❖ Success Principle 37

Self-Efface and Praise

Zen Buddhist monks would have proclaimed Roddey Burdine an instant roshi because he had apparently so completely destroyed his ego. To hear him tell it, he was responsible for none of the success of his business.

Again and again Burdine could be heard publicly saying that "one of the things that a man has to learn in business is how little he can do by himself and that when he finds this out, he begins to look around for people to do what he can't."

To those who knew him, Burdine's modesty would have come as no surprise. But they would have said that he had simply learned from experience and had faced facts from all of his years in business.

Burdine mastered the flip side of the self-effacing equation as well. He not only eschewed praise for himself, he never missed a chance to give the spotlight and credit to others.

A born psychologist, R. B. instinctively knew how much people want and need approbation, especially on the job. So, he was lavish in his praise of those who worked for his company. He never indulged incompetence or negativity for a minute, of course. And he never gave recognition unless it was deserved. But he knew that public recognition, in most cases even more than money, was the greatest motivator of employees.

Roddey Burdine was committed to keeping productive people working at Burdines. Beyond giving employees his own ad hoc pats on the back, he established a lavish system of company recognition for success and longevity, including monetary rewards. He believed that, to be fair, he had to let employees know through what hoops they had to jump legitimately to earn recognition.

Principle 37
Self-Efface and Praise

Applying this Principle to My Business Success

150   *You Can't Go Wrong By Doing It Right*

Burdines Archives

How do you get adults into your store? By creating something their children can't resist, of course. The genius of the Snow Princess was not just that it was the perfect trap, but that everybody also loved being reeled in by it. Served in the downtown Tea Room, the ice cream extravaganza was every little girl's (and little boy's) delight. A little ice cream went a long way in the sub-tropics.

❖ Success Principle 38

Reach Parents Through Their Children

The most successful strategies in war and peace are oblique. Combatants or negotiators who aim for their adversaries head on usually give away their hand too soon and suffer debilitating concussions, if not outright defeat. It is equally the case in marketing. The most effective efforts are never what they appear to be on the surface.

Perhaps Burdines' most lethal attraction for bringing the distaff side of every family in Miami into the store, where they could shop 'til they dropped, was the Snow Princess, a seductive royal of ice cream served in its downtown Tea Room and the sine qua non of every good little girl who ever knew the phrase "Mommy, please may I have…I've been good." Concocted of vanilla ice cream, little silver candy balls, and whipped cream topped with a china doll, Her Highness became a tradition that ensured a steady flow of little children bringing their parents back to the store time and again.

The Snow Princess had all of the ingredients of a perfect gimmick to attract children. First, it had an element of exotic, if not forbidden, fruit about it, suggesting the winter north of sleds, toboggans, and ice skating about which the boys and girls of Florida sunshine could only dream. Second, it was sweet, eventually became messy, and could be played with — to the delight of every minor and the chagrin of most adults. And finally, it could be used as a weapon through which parents could control children:

"If you're good, I'll buy you a Snow Princess, but only if you're good."

So, by selling a form of snow in Miami, Burdines created a marketing gimmick that produced the rare result of satisfying everyone — and establishing the kind of tradition that kept grown-ups flocking to its store on the heels of children. And the beauty of it was that hardly anybody realized the subtle seduction to which they were giving in — or would have cared, had they figured it out.

Principle 38
Reach Parents Through Their Children

Applying this Principle to My Business Success

_____

_____

_____

_____

_____

_____

_____

_____

_____

_____

_____

_____

_____

Historical Museum of Southern Florida

Look in the window and see only shoes, and you couldn't work at Burdines. Look in the window and see the basis for building a possible lifelong relationship with a customer, and you begin to think like William and Roddey Burdine.

❖ Success Principle 39

Make It Better

If gold medals were given for making things better for customers, Burdines would have won one in every Olympiad. Like a masochist doing a tap dance on a bed of nails, the store relished every opportunity to show how much it cared about fixing something that broke or otherwise disappointed its clients.

No matter how abrasive or infantile a patron might become or even how blameless the store might be, Burdines became Clara Barton, Florence Nightingale, and Mother Teresa all rolled into one. It knew that once people had been helped out of a jam, they would be ambassadors for the store forever — or until it let them down.

Situations like the following were not uncommon: Once, "a customer who had purchased a large piece of luggage discovered after packing it, and getting all set for a trip abroad, that she had no key. Burdines sent a key to her home by taxi, but the key would not work. So, the store then sent another similar piece of luggage with keys and helped the woman repack."

In 1936, Burdines announced a new advertising policy to police its own advertising and promotions. It offered to pay cash to the first customer who could point out a misleading statement about its merchandise in its advertising.

No matter what the circumstances, Burdines' strategy was the same: "Kill 'em with kindness." They were wise enough to know that people who have spent their good money feel robbed when something goes wrong. They want someone to compensate them for their discomfort, pain, embarrassment, or inconvenience. And to a fault, Burdines always knew how to make it better.

Principle 39
Make It Better

Applying this Principle to My Business Success

Historical Museum of Southern Florida

The frontier trading post at the left is William Burdine's first store in Miami, located on Avenue D, now South Miami Avenue. Horse-drawn carriages dot the landscape.

A far cry from the sophisticated Burdines department stores of later years, at this location, W. M. catered to customers like Native Americans, pioneer families, soldier hold-overs from the Spanish-American War, and soldiers of one kind of fortune or another. At the time, the population of Miami was about 700-1,000.

❖ Success Principle 40

Make Your Business Your Life

If there had been eight days in every week, William Burdine would have kept his first store in Miami open on each of them and for as late as he profitably could do business. As it happens, he stayed open every night until 10 p.m. and on Saturdays until midnight.

Burdines may have had the outward appearance of a business run by gentlemen in a gentlemanly fashion, but it required dedication and rigor from all of its employees. If you wanted to be anything more than just an hourly worker, your life had to be your work, and your work had to be your life.

The company's unwritten motto easily could have been "Business first, last, and always" — and everyone knew it. No one got ahead who was not consumed by his work, and no one made a pretense to sugarcoat what it took to be advanced within the corporation.

George Whitten, the only non-family member to become president of Burdines while it was family owned, knew from personal experience that if employees wanted to be promoted they had to pay "a price," especially by giving up their personal lives. He made no bones about the success formula for advancing within the organization: "ingenuity in uncovering new and better ways to apply one's talent and overcome obstacles, and personal sacrifice in the matter of time and energy. Hard driving, continuous work, the courage to make decisions, the scouring honesty of never fooling oneself about himself are among the requirements. Inability or unwillingness to subordinate personal interests to the interests of the store prevents many individuals from moving up."

Principle 40
Make Your Business Your Life

Applying this Principle to My Business Success

from the collection of Patti B. Phipps

A youthful Roddey Burdine, Sr. is pictured above slightly to the right of the middle in a straw hat between two young men smoking cigars. Typically, he seems to be avoiding publicity for publicity's sake, more intent upon playing checkers or some other board game than interested in being captured full face by the camera.

❖ Success Principle 41

Splash and Stunt, Slip and Slide

Roddey Burdine conducted his business the way Fred Astaire danced — with grace and ease. He was born with stagemanship, one of the most important elements in his success. Even though he was low-keyed and avoided the limelight, he seems to have been a frustrated performer and to have relished a degree of public presence.

Even after R. B. became a buyer for Burdines, he entertained the thought of becoming a musician rather than staying in business with his father. So, in 1909, when he went to New York on vacation, he actually spent his time playing his cornet in a rathskeller across from the Hay Market. Ultimately, he returned to the family business, of course.

R. B. cultivated a strong public image so that he could put the weight of his character and personality to work for the benefit of his business. He would have been frank in admitting, and regretting, that perception is at least as important as substance — in life, and certainly in business. And in the same breath, he would have acknowledged that if you want to win in the game of life, you have to master the rules. In other words, in addition to being a successful businessman, he looked like and played the part of one.

Had anyone asked him, he would unabashedly have replied, "If you are going to be a success and want to be known as such, show people that you already are one." R. B. had flair. Always dapper, he charmed everyone who dealt with him. He inspired confidence in others and was a natural leader. Throughout his life, he seemed not only destined for center stage, he captured it.

Like every tap dancer, Burdine knew that the public relished some splash and a stunt or two to peak their interest. Like a fox-trotter, he knew when it was time simply to slip and side. But above all, he was astute enough to understand that the head of any business is inseparable from it and that, to be successful, he consciously had to create an image that inspired people's confidence in him.

Principle 41
Splash and Stunt, Slip and Slide

Applying this Principle to My Business Success

Historical Museum of Southern Florida

For all of his outward, easy-going manner, the mature Roddey Burdine was a strong-willed, determined businessman, who was not afraid of making decisions — or of accepting responsibility for having made them, right or wrong.

❖ Success Principle 42

Don't Be Afraid To Be Autocratic

Both William Murrah Burdine and his son Roddey were benevolent dictators, but not at the same time. When Burdines was a family-owned business, there never was room at the top for more than one — and everyone knew it. When decisions needed to be made, there wasn't a lot of hemming and hawing, and there certainly weren't lots of committees. When executives did consider important matters as a group, everyone knew who had the power — and the ultimate responsibility. So much for participatory management — and for passing the buck.

Without a doubt, Roddey learned how to be an autocrat from his father, a man refreshingly free of gnawing gray areas of doubt and indecision. Shortly after his father's death, when Roddey became president of Burdines, he recognized that his business had to grow, and he was not about to let anyone or anything stand in his way.

Apparently, when the plans for the Burdines' "skyscraper" were under discussion, his brother Freeman, an attorney and store corporate officer, objected to them. Roddey is reported to have told his brother that he had not come to see him for advice but to have the necessary papers drawn up to facilitate the expansion. "Attorneys have only to know the law," he is supposed to have said. "Merchants must have brains."

The autocratic gene in the Burdine line was defective, however. After Roddey's death, William, Jr. became president of Burdines in name only. With no interest in business and enough money to allow him to live as a recluse in the Everglades, "Willie" did not even care to go to work, let alone take responsibility for making decisions. Ultimately, a non-family member replaced him.

To be successful, the Burdines always recognized that lines of authority had to be unabashedly clear — to them. In the name of democracy and team-building, no amount of management theory would ever have justified the running of their corporation by the executive equivalent of a headless horseman.

Principle 42
Don't Be Afraid To Be Autocratic

Applying this Principle to My Business Success

Florida State Archives

Burdines set out to establish itself as a store that made fashion, elegance, and refinement available to sophisticated, as well as average, women. It identified and then pursued a certain niche. The rooftop of the downtown Miami Burdines is the stage for a revue of the lastest fashions in this photograph from 1929, the year in which the store began to promote its trademark "Sunshine Fashions." Thereafter, it set the pace in tropical style not only in South Florida but nationwide.

❖ Success Principle 43

Know Your Niche — and Fill It

By today's "let-it-all-hang-out, anything goes" standard of dress, language, and general demeanor, Roddey Burdine's stores would have appeared formal, stiff, and even a bit condescending. They did not welcome uncontrolled children running through their aisles, drooling on display cases or otherwise disturbing the peace. And they certainly expected adults to be on their best behavior. Burdines was not about to be swept away by America's unwashed multitudes.

On the other hand, Queen Elizabeth II and any in her blue-blood retinue would have felt right at home, not to mention the myriads of ordinary Americans who gravitate to stores that cater as much to creating atmosphere as to purveying merchandise.

There was a kind of hush all over the stores. They were bastions of Victorian and Southern sensibility. Burdines knew what share of the market it wanted to attract, and it didn't send mixed messages.

Roddey Burdine set out to create an image of refinement, sophistication, and civility because he knew that there were people who wanted shopping to be as much a social occasion as a matter of practical necessity. He wanted to raise the level of people's everyday lives, to give them something special to look forward to, and to treat them with respect. He probably said on more than one occasion, "We want to make every woman feel like a queen for a day."

R. B. would have been the first to say, "Know your general market, decide upon the niche that you want to fill, and stick with your strategy. Don't try to be all things to all people, and never stoop to conquer."

Principle 43
Know Your Niche — and Fill It

Applying this Principle to My Business Success

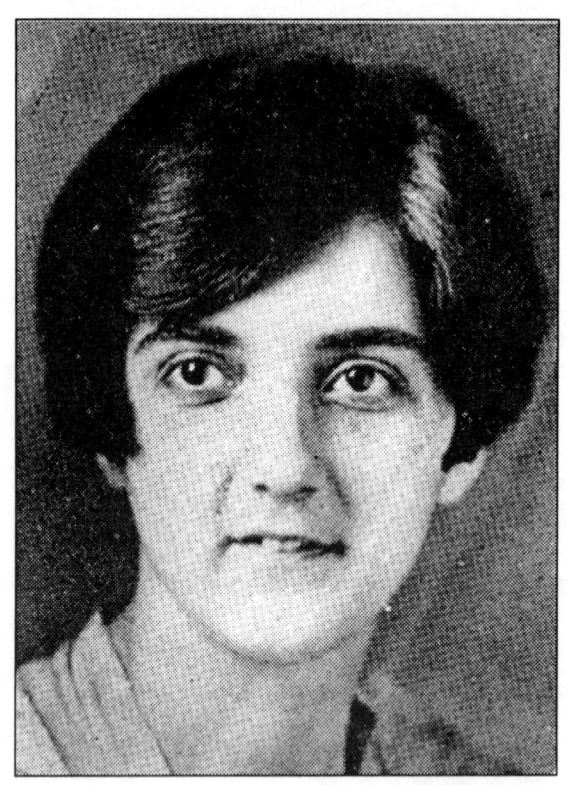

Burdines Archives

In August 1926, Mrs. Marguerite S. Behrenhausen was singled out in the Burdines' newsletter because she had sold the most merchandise in the May storewide sale. Her career in retail began when she was just in her teens in Reading, Pennsylvania. Starting as a messenger, she soon became a saleslady and, after nine years, worked her way up to assistant to the buyer — before working in sales at Burdines.

❖ Success Principle 44

Get Thy Hands Dirty

Today, too many people are caught up in a frenzied pursuit of immediate success. They are so conditioned to instant gratification, that when they enter the workforce or go into business, they expect to rise to the top overnight. The notion that anyone should have to pay his dues and put in her time is alien to upwardly mobile would-be entrepreneurs, executives, and captains of industry. They want multi-million-dollar salaries and generous stock options now, because they feel that they are entitled to them.

When William Burdine made his son Roddey sweep out the store and do other menial chores after he had been expelled from school, he was clearly punishing him. But he was also sending other messages to his son: honest work is good therapy; developing a proper work ethic has a way of straightening out people in every aspect of their life; and there is dignity in learning how to do any job well.

So, it should come as no surprise that Burdines sent a subtle message to all of its employees that no job was too low and no task was too demeaning — even for its owners. William stooped to do any number of back-breaking jobs and expected others to do the same if called upon. Even after Roddey formally came into the business, he enjoyed no special privilege, but was expected to start at the bottom of the ladder and to learn all aspects of operating the store.

Apprenticeship was the vehicle to success, not theoretical knowledge. Employees were expected to learn on the job and to demonstrate not only what they knew but how well they knew it by producing results over time. And they understood that their success and advancement would take time, if it ever came, and that no one should be in a hurry.

Principle 44
Get Thy Hands Dirty

Applying this Principle to My Business Success

Historical Museum of Southern Florida

These first winter visitors to Biscayne Bay in the 1890's and others like them probably would have been among William Burdine's early patrons. Along with baubles, bangles, and beads, Burdine had much to offer them to acclimate them to the sub-tropics.

❖ Success Principle 45

Look for the Chicken Before the Egg

Most people would say that to be a success in business, you have to have a great idea or the right product or service. William Burdine would have said, "I wasn't a real success until I found the right location." In fact, his whole life can be said to have been a search for the perfect place in which to do business.

Central Florida and the lure of "Orange Gold" had led Burdine to leave his native Mississippi when he was forty-seven. After he lost two citrus crops in as many years, he became first a partner in a dry goods store in Bartow, Florida, and then its sole proprietor. But when business was slower than he expected it to be, he began to look around for new opportunities.

The hot spot of the decade of the 1890's turned out to be south of Burdine in Miami, where he found a city on the verge of emerging from sub-tropical swamps and a population in need of precisely what he had to offer.

The lesson in all this is a simple one: you may have the best product or service, but no market in which to sell it; in which case, you will not be able to run a successful business. On the other hand, you may not have a particularly great idea, an innovative product, a worthwhile service, or even the vaguest notion of what you want to sell, but if you find a sizeable enough (or growing) market and study what it needs, you may well become a great success.

W. M. instinctively knew the answer to the conundrum, "Which comes first, the chicken or the egg?" because he had no intention of laying one in business.

Principle 45
Look for the Chicken Before the Egg

Applying this Principle to My Business Success

182   *You Can't Go Wrong By Doing It Right*

Historical Museum of Southern Florida

Generations of women remembered their first shopping excursion to Burdines, their first party dress, their first high heels, their first Snow Princess — in short, the special milestones in their lives, big and small.

❖ Success Principle 46

Always Remember

"Success in life, as well as in business, is in the details," Roddey Burdine would have said. "Always remember the little things that are important to others — the people you work with, your customers, and the people in your personal life.

"Remember to show your co-workers that you care about them. Be genuinely interested in their family. Remember their children's names and where they are in life. Congratulate them on the birth of their children and grandchildren, and remember to show your sympathy when sadness enters their lives.

"Remember the names of your customers. You can't expect people to give you their business over and over again if you don't make an effort to remember who they are. No one wants to be forgotten. Remember their birthdays. We all celebrate major holidays, but to many people, their birthday is their special day, and anything you do to acknowledge it will be appreciated.

"Remember the colors that your customers like and the styles that they prefer. Keep track of what they have bought from you in a small notebook, so that when we have a sale, you can write to them personally, inviting them to benefit from it. Look for merchandise that you know will appeal to them.

"Read the local news in the papers diligently. Many of our customers are well known and are written about in the press. If something good happens to them, remember to write and congratulate them. If something ill befalls them, don't forget to express your condolences or your wishes for their speedy recovery — to show them that they are in your thoughts and that they mean more to you than just a sale.

"Remember never to take those closest to you, your family and friends, for granted. Pay every attention to their smallest needs and wants.

"Remember to take the time to follow up on even what may appear to be the most insignificant details and your effort will be repaid with riches at every level, for the more you remember others, the more you yourself will be remembered."

Principle 46
Always Remember

Applying this Principle to My Business Success

Historical Museum of Southern Florida

Burdines tried to think of every customer's every need and relished providing every possible convenience. It bent over backwards to make everyone, even non-shoppers, feel at home.

Recalling a time when letter-writing was the preferred form of communication, in the Hibiscus lounge of the downtown Miami store, Burdines provided writing desks for the convenience of busy patrons and others who just needed to find a place to sit right down and write someone else a letter — as though today a retail establishment thought enough to provide free internet access to any of its customers.

(In a remarkable commentary on the honesty of bygone times and the caliber of Burdines' customers, the pens in this picture do not appear to have been tied down to discourage theft.)

❖ Success Principle 47

Make Everybody Happy

"Make all of your customers feel as though they are on the French Riviera when they come into Burdines," Roddey Burdine would have reminded his salespeople.

"Everybody has dreams. Most people want to escape the humdrum of their day-to-day existences for a world in which everything is beautiful and exactly as they imagine it. So, do your best to give everybody who comes into Burdines the experience of perfection.

"Our customers do not just come here to buy things for themselves or others. They want to leave us feeling better about themselves than they did when they came in. If they are looking for a gift, they want to go away believing that they have made the perfect choice, and that the recipient of it will be elated and think happily of them. If they are in the market for something for themselves, they want to know deep down that they have found exactly what they have been looking for. They do not want to leave here feeling as though they have settled for second best — that they can do anywhere. Burdines is different."

Ladies regularly came to Burdines to experience "The Perfect Day." They would start off mid-morning in the beauty salon, having their hair coiffed and their nails manicured. Next, they would meet friends for luncheon in the Tea Room. And afterwards, they would spend the rest of the afternoon shopping. They would emerge from Burdines in late afternoon, looking good and feeling like royalty, subconsciously reassured that when their most recent hit of euphoria wore off, they would be back for more.

Principle 47
Make Everybody Happy

Applying this Principle to My Business Success

Burdines Archives

Born to W. M.'s first wife Georgie Ann Davis, John M. Burdine (1874-1951) was the first Burdine son to go into business with his father. The heir apparent to the stewardship of the company, John shocked his family when he left Burdines to go into business with Mrs. Eva Quarterman. She had worked for W. M. in Bartow and had even pulled up stakes, moving with the Burdines to Miami in 1898. Establishing Burdine and Quarterman, John actually went into competition with his father.

Though the causes of the break are not fully documented anywhere, it is reasonable to surmise that the combination of John's marriage to Eva Quarterman's daughter Pauline and Mrs. Quarterman's business and personal ambitions were the major catalysts for John's striking out on his own. Burdine and Quarterman did not survive the economic bust of 1926. Eventually, John Burdine went into the insurance business.

❖ Success Principle 48

Never Depend Upon the Weather or People Who Say They'll Get Back to You within Ten Days

Someone once said, "Don't invest in anything that eats or needs water." Having seen his orange groves destroyed in the two devastating frosts of 1894 and 1895, William M. Burdine was inclined to add, "Don't go into a business that depends upon the weather."

Experience had taught W.M. bitter lessons of self-reliance, that people should not be foolish enough to think that they can count on anything or anyone outside of themselves — even his son. John Burdine, who first had gone into business with his father in Bartow and opened the store in Miami, later left Burdines and started a competing business with his mother-in-law, who had been a Burdines' employee.

Of course, when he moved to Miami, W. M. did and did not follow his own advice. Obviously, his trading post was indoors, so he was protected from the elements. But ironically, the city in which he had relocated depended upon the weather, both in its immediate locale as well as around the country, for its economic survival. An opportunist, William Burdine always had a supply of umbrellas for sale to save unprepared customers from the cloud-bursts, of course, but he knew that he had to secure the future of his business in major ways by finding promising alternative venues.

Even in the early years in Miami, W. M. recognized the importance of diversifying as a general business strategy. For example, he was wary of relying upon a sole source for his merchandise. And he knew how crucial it would be eventually to expand by replicating his business in Miami into other nearby markets.

As for "people who say they'll get back to you within ten days," to Burdine they were less reliable even than the weather. He trusted no one he hadn't known for years.

Such lessons were not lost on his son Roddey, who, in addition to being schooled by his father, had an almost constitutional aversion to dependence upon others. Had he not found himself in the heart of a growing region, he instinctively would have extended the reach of his business, if only to carry him through those inevitable sub-tropical rainy days.

Principle 48
Never Depend Upon the Weather or People Who Say They'll Get Back to You within Ten Days

Applying this Principle to My Business Success

194   You Can't Go Wrong By Doing It Right

Historical Museum of Southern Florida

In December 1938, a large chunk of Flagler Street frontage (the Biscayne Hotel) had been chopped away for a Burdines' expansion. After World War II, the remainder of the hotel was torn down to make room for yet another addition that today is the SE corner of Flagler Street and Miami Avenue.

❖ Success Principle 49

Be an Anarchist

Today, American businesses, especially retailers, have lost most, if not all, of their humanity. The bureaucrats have won. They successfully have created a firewall of rules and regulations between themselves and the public, routinely read their customers the riot act, and otherwise find ways to wiggle out of being responsive to individual consumer's needs.

At least for the short term, the sheer size and market share of some corporations apparently guarantee the health of their profits. It appears to be a seller's market that they are free to exploit and abuse as long as they can get away with it.

What these businesses have failed to understand is what Burdines mastered from the start: No rule should stand in the way of satisfying a customer's needs; rules are made to be broken; and anarchists in sales are those who are most successful.

Neither William nor Roddey Burdine ever would have accepted the excuse that a corporate rule stood in the way of a salesperson's making a sale. "Customers do not want to hear that there is any reason why they cannot obtain the merchandise they want from us when they want it," both Burdines would have insisted. "They want us to deliver the goods. We made the rules. We can break them. It is our job to go out on a limb. There is no policy or procedure of this business that can be justified if it stands between us and making a sale, and anyone who thinks so is invited to work for our competitors."

**Principle 49
Be an Anarchist**

Applying this Principle to My Business Success

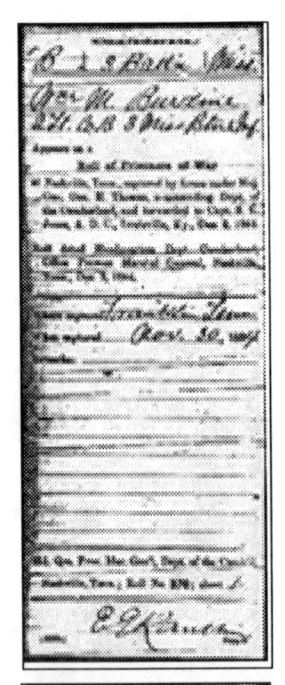

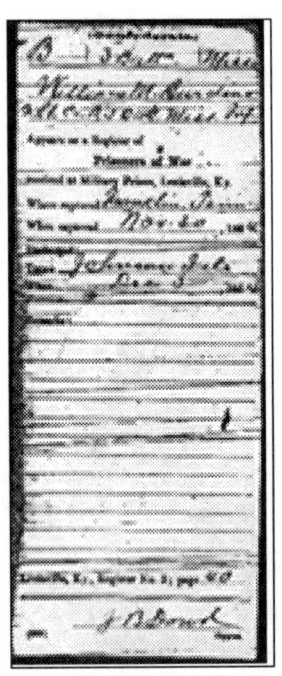

The National Archives

W. M. Burdine was a soldier in the Confederate Army from 1861 until 1865. (From top left to right) As his military records show, his name appears on the Roll of Prisoners of War as one who was captured at the Battle of Franklin on November 30, 1864. On December 3, he was sent from the military prison at Louisville, Kentucky to Johnson Isle prison off the coast of Sandusky, Ohio. (Lower left) Finally, on June 16, 1865, two months after the end of the Civil War, he was released from prison after he agreed to swear an oath of allegiance to the Federal government.

❖ Success Principle 50

Learn to Live with Failing

It is only fitting that the last Burdine success principle be about failure, specifically about giving people the freedom to fail. After all, psychology and common sense tell us that only those people who are able to fail can succeed, that you can't enjoy the one without experiencing the other.

Failure played a major role in William Burdine's life. He lived with minor failures, as everyone does. His decision to move to Homeland, Florida was a failure, as were his failures as a citrus grower and a retailer in Bartow. But more importantly, he lived under a complex cloud of failure that would never lift.

William Burdine was the product of a failed generation, and he succeeded precisely (perhaps, only) because he and his peers saw themselves as failures and didn't sugarcoat it. He never got over participating in the grand failure of the Civil War as a Confederate soldier and lived with the humiliation of that experience for the rest of his life — and the need to compensate for it, rather than to wish it away.

What set William Burdine apart from most people who fail was his naivete, his willingness to accept responsibility for failing without calling it something else.

Today, people who have the benefit of modern theories of behavior, projection, and transference are adept at using verbal gyrations conveniently to differentiate the agents of an action from the act itself. Typically, they try to counsel people into feeling good by saying that they are not failures, but they simply do things that do not succeed.

Burdine had a robust appreciation for failure, because he knew its value unadulterated. He would have been the first to say that people should hold onto their gnawing sense of incompletion, disappointment, and self-rejection rather than look for a therapeutic way to neutralize them. He knew that the guilt that people feel because they have failed prodded them to succeed in other ways and that to deny or otherwise rationalize failure was to remove the most effective spur to success.

The last word on what made William Murrah Burdine a success and set in motion his family and business success is simply that he saw himself as a failure and spent his life trying to overcome it.

Principle 50
Learn to Live with Failing

Applying this Principle to My Business Success

Part II

✧

The Burdine Success Story

Burdines Archives

William Murrah Burdine, Sr.
(1843-1911)

At 5' 8," with dark hair, a fair complexion, and steel-grey eyes, W. M. Burdine, the founder of the stores that bear his name, was a giant of a man. Born in 1843, in Monroe County (Mississippi), at 18, he joined the Confederate Army. Wounded at the Battles of Shiloh and Murfreesboro, he was taken prisoner at the Battle of Franklin and incarcerated on Johnson's Island, Ohio for 6^1/$_2$ months — until shortly after the Civil War.

Twice married, he was the father of seven children who survived into adulthood — three by his first wife, Georgie Ann Davis, who died at age 30 in Verona (Mississippi) and four by his second wife, Mollie Taylor Freeman. Moving first to Homeland (Bartow), Florida in 1890, W. M. relocated his business and family to Miami, Florida in 1898, setting in motion one of South Florida's most prominent and enduring family success stories.

By today's standards for corporate conduct, the chain of events responsible for the Burdine business success story begins most improbably in the middle of the nineteenth century in the lush rolling hills of northeast Mississippi, where William Murrah Burdine was born and spent the better part of his first forty-seven years. He grew up in and was molded by the antebellum South. Nearly everything that was really decisive in his life and that shaped his ultimate success in Florida happened to him long before he arrived there.

First of all, the quest for adventure that would shake Burdine out of his comfortable life and eventually embolden him to move to Miami ran in his blood. Born in 1843 in rural Mississippi, he grew up during the Age of Pioneers, with the memory and knowledge of his rugged, itinerant ancestors part of the integral lessons of his early life. He had heard the grand stories of their trek across America, ritually settling in and pulling up stakes in one untamed wilderness after another.

For almost thirty years, his forebears had made their own way, cutting a path from Virginia, through North and South Carolina, Alabama and Georgia, until finally making Mississippi their home sometime before 1818. Burdine roots in Mississippi eventually ran deep. The family lived peaceably with the Chicasaw Indians and with others of the earliest settlers who in later years arrived from the eastern seaboard in covered wagons, forging through the wilderness, wading through water, and otherwise negotiating dirt trails and inhospitable streams, as the Burdines once had.

Those lessons of resilience and detachment, self-reliance and determination subconsciously shaped William's core values and beliefs, as they would have those of any impressionable youth. Above all, throughout his entire life, William Burdine knew that he was from strong, pioneer stock that cleared its own way, claimed its stake, and stuck with whatever they did.

Secondly, the Civil War had everything to do with shaping William's character and later life, including even his eventual success in business. In 1861, when he was only eighteen, he went to war as a soldier in the Confederate Army. After knowing nothing but the peace and security of his early years in the hills of rural Mississippi, with the outbreak of the Civil War, in what seemed to be just a single horrifying instant, Burdine was forced to come of age in the most turbulent of times.

From 1861 to 1865, he fought in almost every major battle of the Civil War — at Murfreesboro, Chickamanga, Shiloh, Perrysville, Missionary Ridge, and numerous others. For four years, day after day, he lived among the dead and dying in a helter-skelter of horror, the crossfire of carnage, and in frenzied scenes of human annihilation, in which bodies were dismembered, brains were strewn on the ground before him, and the sight of blood was everywhere. He heard the cries of maimed young men writhing in pain that no one could ease. He choked from the suffocating smoke of gunfire and the stench of mass slaughter. He had grown accustomed to watching his friends and fellow soldiers die right in front of him, to looking into the upturned faces of the dead, and later, in a final indignity, to seeing their bodies grow swollen and disfigured from the heat. He himself was twiced wounded in battle, but lived to go back into the fight and tell about it.

Next to dying in combat, Burdine and his fellow soldiers would have said among themselves that the mortification of being taken prisoner was a soldier's worst nightmare. During the Battle of Franklin, he experienced that truth firsthand, for when he was only twenty-one, he was taken a prisoner of war. Deprived of his personal freedom for the first time in his life, William Murrah Burdine went from being the proud son of John Fletcher Burdine, Jr. and citizen of Mississippi to something less than a human being, nothing more than a name, number, and a spoil of war in the eyes of the enemy.

After he was taken into custody, in chains, William Burdine was eventually brought to Johnson's Island off the coast of Sandusky, Ohio, where, among other things, he endured the bitterest winter of his life — relentless temperatures far below zero, the bone-chilling wind coming through the walls, and no possibility of keeping warm.

Still, all of the external hardship that Burdine suffered was nothing compared to the debasement of his spirit. He saw his fellow southerners, once-proud officers and soldiers alike, humiliated. For six and one-half months, he lived among half-men in sub-human conditions, overpowered by the stench of human waste. The food was barely edible. Food rations were cut so severely, that inmates began to kill and eat rats in order to survive. The boredom was palpable. Like everyone else, he had to fight depression. Terrorized, he knew that even a slight infraction of the rules could have led to his being shot.

208 You Can't Go Wrong By Doing It Right

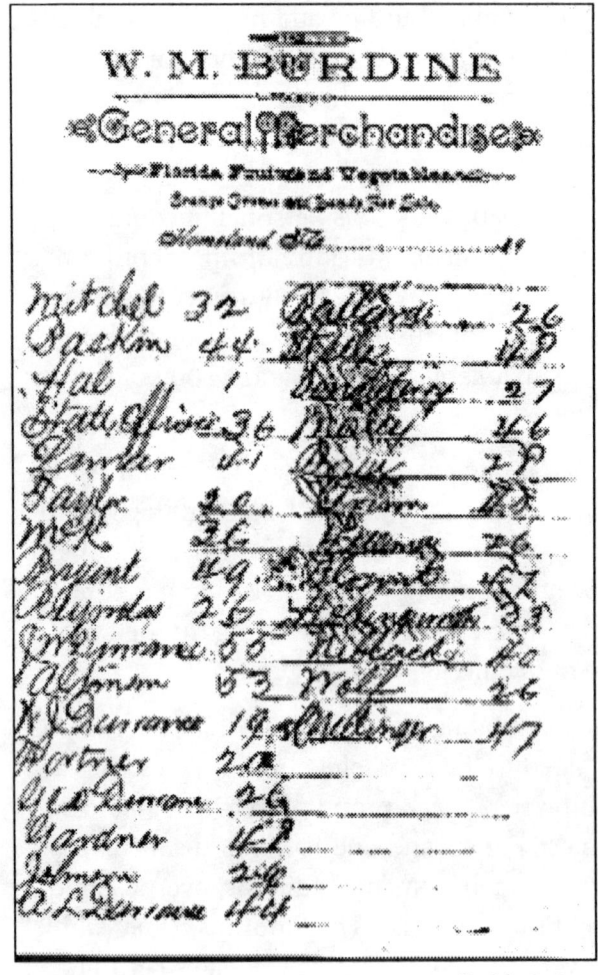

Dr. John B. Crum

First Business in Bartow

Having moved to Homeland (Florida) in 1890, William Burdine entered the citrus business, and also appears to have sold orange groves and land. It is unclear precisely what this undated ledger is recording. Perhaps it is an accounting of the number of bushels of fruit picked by various laborers.

Burdine was still imprisoned when news came of the end of the Civil War, though there was little for him to celebrate in the defeat of the South. A week later, he learned that Abraham Lincoln had been assassinated. On June 16, 1865, he did what he never thought he would have to do when the war began: he signed an oath of allegiance to the Federal government. With just a stroke of a pen, the worst ordeal of his life ended and he was free to return home to Mississippi.

If signing the oath of allegiance ultimately made him a free man in the eyes of his captors and the Federal government, surely William Burdine's deep religious convictions and personal resolve had to have been what gave him the inner freedom that kept him alive throughout his ordeal, in spite of the hardships that he had had to endure. Every day of the six and a half months that he had spent in prison he lived from moment to moment, never certain that he would ever see his loved ones or friends again or that he would survive his ordeal to tell about it.

Burdine emerged from the Civil War a changed man, mature far beyond his twenty-two years — reliving at once in his imagination the conflicting recollections of a youthful tranquility that had so suddenly given way to epic bloodshed, strengthened by the knowledge that he had been able to survive but mortified by the thought of how many others did not, and steeled against the challenges of living, like others of his generation who had come face-to-face with their own death and the death of others.

For William Burdine, the war would never become a distant recollection like a chapter in a textbook to be memorized for a lesson in American history. It was real life to him, never to be forgotten, no matter how hard he

Florida State Archives

"After the Freeze"
January 29, 1895

This photograph captures one of the circumstances that set in motion William Burdine's eventual success in Miami and the founding of Burdines Department Stores. It shows a citrus grove destroyed by the freeze of 1895 — the same frost that devastated the Burdine groves in Homeland.

Had it not been for the freezes of 1894 and 1895, W. M. would not have gone into the dry goods business with Mr. Payne or later dissolved that partnership to form Burdine and Son in Bartow. Chances are, if he still had been in the citrus business in 1898, he never would have gone south to Miami, even with the prospects for business looking as good as they did.

might try. It put his values to the test, showed him how to survive and thrive, even in face of death. He emerged from it one of the lost generation of southerners whose lives abruptly were changed beyond recognition, but who learned how to overcome cultural obliteration, how to start over and over again if necessary, and how to look upon the American landscape as a vast canvas of limitless possibility even in a sea of hardship. The war refined William Murrah Burdine's character. Ironically, the same experience that at one level took away his humanity actually made him a human being by teaching him the things in life and the values in himself and in others that really matter.

But if Burdine thought that his travails were over when he left prison, he would soon discover that day-to-day life back home would continue to test his endurance. The devastation that he found in Mississippi when he returned would have been impossible to imagine when he left, for it was almost impossible to believe, even though he saw it with his own eyes.

Everywhere he looked he felt the haunting presence of the dead and the injured, the terrorized, and the defeated. Civilians had had to suffer the brunt of battle close to home — houses turned into makeshift surgeries, gardens made into funeral plots. Living in Mississippi after the war was a reality of enduring not only defeat but humiliation, without money or the prospect of earning a living. The area was reduced to an ugly poverty and to seething conflicts and social undercurrents that broke through the surface between freed slaves who were wielding political, economic, and social power for the first time and their former masters who had been broken and defeated.

Polk County Historical Association

Burdine & Son
(Main Street, Bartow, Florida, 1897)

W. M. Burdine launched his career in retail not in Miami, but in Bartow, Florida. Dr. John Burdine Crum, his grandson, identifies the store at the left of this picture that is partially obscured by the large oak tree as the site of Payne and Burdine, the precursor of Burdine and Son. It is on the northeast corner of Main Street and North Central Avenue.

Writing in the Polk County Historical Quarterly, Dr. Crum observes that W. M. Burdine and Henry Payne formed their partnership in a dry goods store on April 22, 1896. Lasting just fourteen months, the firm of Payne and Burdine was superseded by Burdine and Son on August 18, 1897. The son referred to was John M. Burdine, one of two sons born to W. M.'s first wife, Georgie Ann Davis, who died in 1880 in Verona, Mississippi.

William Murrah Burdine had had to grow up young and in a hurry. He knew what it was to lose everything, to see his life altered beyond recognition in very way, and he resolved never to let that happen again. Against the turbulent backdrop of reconstructing the South, Burdine set about to restore his life — and did so with more than modest success. He clerked for a small dry goods store in Verona, Mississippi, but then, with $500 that his father-in-law gave him and his wife, he opened a drug business. By all accounts he prospered; by one account, he even grew rich. For the next twenty-five years, he settled in, raised a family, suffered the loss of his first wife and two young children, remarried, and carried on. For him, life had settled into productive, predictable patterns.

But in early 1890, for the second time in his life, William Murrah Burdine left his Mississippi hills, this time accompanied by his wife and six children — and this time, as it would turn out, for good. Like his ancestors, at forty-seven, W. M. set his sights on a distant horizon and broke out of the mold in which he found himself. Partly for reasons of his health and partly to pursue a unique business opportunity, he moved to Florida.

A farmer in his youth before the Civil War, long before he became a businessman, William Burdine reverted to type in middle age. He was caught up in the frenzy of the rush for "Orange Gold." Like others, he believed that with the opening of Florida's "northern territories," there was money to be made in growing and selling citrus. In a major leap of faith, he moved to Central Florida, to Homeland outside of Bartow, near Tampa, into the frenzy of a community developing around the citrus industry. By the last decade of the nineteenth century, Bartow spelled "opportunity" to anyone

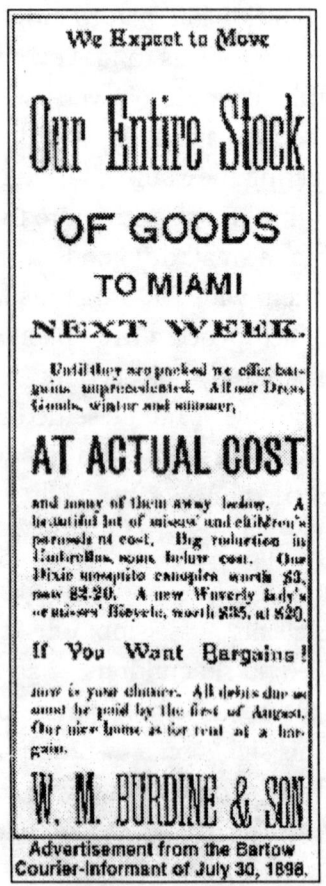

> **We Expect to Move**
>
> ## Our Entire Stock
>
> ### OF GOODS
>
> ### TO MIAMI
>
> ### NEXT WEEK.
>
> Until they are packed we offer bargains unprecedented. All our Dress Goods, winter and summer,
>
> ### AT ACTUAL COST
>
> and many of them away below. A beautiful lot of misses' and children's parasols at cost. Big reduction in Umbrellas, some below cost. Our Dixie mosquito canopies worth $3, now $2.20. A new Waverly Lady's or misses' Bicycle, worth $35, at $20.
>
> ### If You Want Bargains!
>
> now is your chance. All debts due us must be paid by the first of August. Our nice home is for rent at a bargain.
>
> ## W. M. BURDINE & SON
>
> Advertisement from the Bartow Courier-Informant of July 30, 1898.

Polk County Historical Association

Leaving Bartow

Eight years after moving to Florida, the Burdines picked up stakes again. When the prospects of business in Miami exceeded W. M.'s original projections, he decided not just to open a branch store in South Florida, but to close W. M. Burdine & Son in Bartow and move his family to Miami. This advertisement not only announces the closing of the business in Bartow, but also mentions that the Burdine residence is available for rent. Perhaps W. M. was reluctant to sell his home until he had a better sense of his ultimate success in Miami.

who was wise enough to read the signs. The population boomed. Retail business was brisk. There was even a shortage of residential and commercial space for rent.

So, William Burdine moved his family into the rough and tumble life of a frontier town, in which pistol-shooting was almost as common as citrus-picking. He bought land in Homeland, built a two-story house, planted orange groves, and appeared to be settling into the routine of a quietly prosperous life.

But then, two devastating freezes — in 1894 and 1895 — destroyed the Burdine orange groves, along with many others in Central Florida. Never one to become emotional over an investment or to pursue an unprofitable course for long, William became convinced that he had to make a change, the sooner the better.

Before long, with his characteristic resiliency, by early 1896, Burdine went into the dry goods business on Main Street in Bartow, first with a partner and then, a year later, with his son John. The firm of Burdine and Son opened in August 1897.

After less than a year, when business was not as good as Burdine would have wanted it to be, W. M. was already beginning to think of other ways to make a living, when a few hundred miles to the south a second war would present him with the opportunity he was waiting for.

Just six months after Burdine and Son was established in Bartow, on February 15, 1898, the battleship Maine was blown up in the far-off harbor of Havana, Cuba, setting in motion the opening diplomatic and military salvos of the Spanish-American War. Fighting began on May 1, but was

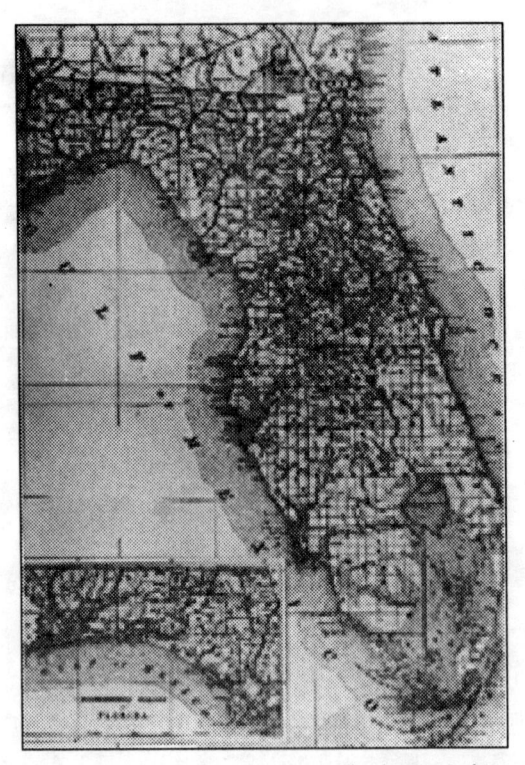

Florida State Archives

Travelling in Florida in the 1890's

Travelling over land or moving a family from place to place in Florida in the 1890's was not something to be taken for granted. There were no major roads sweeping through the state. Flagler's railroad went through to Miami in 1896. But when John M. Burdine went south from Bartow to scout out the business opportunities in Miami, he is supposed to have travelled by wagon, no small feat in those days. John Burdine did not leave an account of his journey in 1898, but Isidor Cohen wrote about his trip in 1896: "At Jupiter the four [in his party] left the boat, to proceed by foot. The horse was the real hero of that trip, for he had to walk railroad ties, cross currents, swim streams and creeks, pulling the two men."(The Miami Daily News, August 13, 1933) over in just ten weeks. As part of the American strategy for invading Spanish Cuba and Puerto Rico, 7,000 troops were sent to Miami, then a village of only about 700 permanent residents, creating the need for a myriad of goods and services and an instant market for savvy businessmen.

A number of prominent businessmen not only read the accounts of the troops in Miami, they read between the lines and concluded that the war spelled opportunity and that South Florida was the place to be. Burdine himself concluded that Miami was "springing up and seemed to have a future."

So, starting in the summer of 1898, an exodus from Bartow began. It was not certain at the outset that the entire Burdine family would move from Miami. Wisely and cautiously, they decided to test the business climate before entirely relocating. By the most probable account of their move south, John M. Burdine, then 24, first left Bartow alone for Miami with merchandise to sell to the troops. Presumably driving his wagon over a difficult terrain on a series of primitive trails — as well as walking, wading through water and mud in some areas, and possibly being ferried across others — he arrived in Miami in the summer of 1898. Shortly thereafter, quiet, resolute, adventurous, and driven, at age 55, William Murrah Burdine once again set out with his family for the greatest challenge of his life.

The late 1890's were the start of the Age of Giants in Miami, when its earliest developers like Julia Tuttle and Henry Flagler were roaming the streets, excavating its landscape, and platting its future — almost at will. They operated on the grandest of scales, literally conceiving of the future of an entire region and, at least for a time, having the resources to carry out their dreams. Everywhere,

Historical Museum of Southern Florida

Miami, 1898

For all of the city's promise, of which he felt certain, at 55, W. M. Burdine clearly was taking a major risk and making a major leap of faith when he moved his family south.

Even allowing for powerlines, this picture of the J.N. Chamberlin house on East Flagler in 1898, the year in which Burdine moved his family to Miami, captures something of the primitiveness of the place.

there was creative energy in the air. Moreover, the kinds of buildings — churches, schools, banks and stores — that tell everyone that a town or village is on the rise were starting to take shape, replacing tents, shacks, and other temporary structures.

To live in Miami, a person had to have stamina to get through today and extra fortitude and vision to plan for tomorrow. It was a time of boundless idealism and energy, the frenzy of a city, indeed a region, unfolding in the first stages of life, beckoning people to it who were willing to risk everything and anything for their personal, as well as a community, dream. Rugged individualists, the savvy pioneers who lived in Miami had a vested interest in ensuring the lasting good fortunes of the city, without which, they knew, their own success could never come about.

Still, Miami was largely waiting to happen in the summer of 1898, little more than wishful thinking in the collective imagination of its earliest pioneers, of which the Burdines would soon form so important a part. Just two years before, the first passengers had arrived on Flagler's brand new Florida East Coast Railroad, that literally opened the region to development. The city had a couple of ginmills but little else to recommend it, unless a person liked hunting, fishing, and bicycle racing.

Even those who had had the fortitude, the vision, and the daring to risk their future in pursuit of Miami's special magic would have to have confessed that those early years were not the city's best. In part, Miami had become a tent city to accommodate the 7,000 soldiers waiting to fight in the war, and they had given the town bad publicity. Bored, assaulted by mosquitoes, and increasingly convinced that they had traipsed to Miami for nothing, because the

Historical Museum of Southern Florida

"Waiting to Invade Cuba"

The 7,000 American troops like these in Miami, armed and poised to invade Spanish Cuba, never got the chance to prove themselves in battle. But they did leave their permanent mark on Miami. Disgruntled because they had to suffer the indignities of a sub-tropical summer in 1898; rowdy by nature and because of prevailing conditions — they upset the delicate balance that always exists between the peaceful and the disorderly in a frontier town. Still, ironically, they were a major catalyst in developing and civilizing South Florida.

Spanish-American War was over almost before it began, the soldiers found all too many anti-social things to do, like swimming naked in the bay, stealing from shopkeepers, taking practice shots at coconuts, and assaulting women.

Even without the soldiers' antics, Miami was a forbidding, untamed wilderness, in which one set of folks wore guns to protect themselves not only against panthers but other people. Already half of the tiny downtown area had burned down on Christmas night in 1896, and for six months in 1899, the city had been quarantined during a yellow fever epidemic.

The story of the Burdines' success in Miami unfolds out of the drama eventually created by the two complementary visions of two different men, a father and his son. William Burdine's vision of what a person was and how he succeeded was based upon sheer grit. He had the capacity to look ahead and to see far beyond other men, but his instincts were grounded in what it took to survive in the present. He also knew how to dig in and apply himself, whatever the cost in time and energy.

William Burdine had been used to making something out of nothing for most of life. So, when he came to Miami, his having to make a fresh start was just another in a series of challenges to his resolve and inventiveness to which he had long been accustomed. He was the foundation-builder, the calm, steady man at the helm. A benevolent autocrat with a pioneering spirit, W. M. never took no, from others, for a final answer, and never said yes unless he meant it. As long as he was alive, there would be only one person in charge at Burdines.

Historical Museum of Southern Florida

Miami Avenue in 1897, just one year before the Burdines moved south, had all of the trappings of a pioneer's wonderland.

When W. M. opened his trading post, he ran it with two employees and family members. Open every night until 10 p.m. and on Saturdays until midnight, the store was a jumble of items. There were no departments and no fancy display cases. Customers had their pick of calicos and overalls, canvas work gloves, neckties and white flannel pants. Merchandise tenuously hung from the ceiling on strings; straw hats were displayed on wire clips. Burdine's stock-in-trade was clothing for men and trading notions and piece goods for the ladies. He carried everything a woman needed to make a dress; in those days, nothing was ready-made. Because of the climate, mosquito net canopies for beds and umbrellas were natural bestsellers.

Burdine bought his stock from drummers, salesmen who traveled to Miami, but he also made two or three buying trips a year to New York. "Sell the best, but keep the price fair," Burdine insisted. It was strictly a cash-and-carry business; but then again, they really didn't need to deliver because all seven hundred residents of Miami lived within walking distance of the store.

Most of Burdine's first customers were Seminole and Miccosuckee Indians, construction workers building the new city, and an assortment of pioneers. The Indians came in single file and shopped in single file, the women carrying their papooses on their backs. Around town, would-be stylish Seminoles sported incongruous derbies, vests, and gold watch chains to complement the ostrich plumes in their headdresses, all of which came from Burdines.

Those early years became the stuff of legend, spawning rustic tales, tall or true, of life in a frontier business — of Indians trading their egret feathers and alligator hides so that they could get cash to buy dry goods at Burdines. By

Burdines Archives

Roddey Bell Burdine, Sr., (1886-1936)

Roddey Burdine, Sr. became the president of Burdines after his father, W. M. died in 1911. Born in Verona, Mississippi in 1886, R. B. was four when he moved to Homeland (Bartow), Florida with his family and twelve when he arrived in Miami.

Dubbed the "Merchant Prince," R. B. is rightly credited with turning the trading post that his father started into the sophisticated chain of department stores of national, indeed international, reputation that Burdines became. He never went to college, but R. B. was born with a marketing instinct, an indomitable will, and an affability that made him a natural success in business and in life.

Often referred to as Miami's "First Citizen," R. B. nonetheless kept a low profile, contributing to civic and charitable causes anonymously, working behind the scenes rather than in the limelight.

one contemporary account, Tiger Charlie, a Seminole, once bought a complete bolt of calico that happened to catch his eye. Reaching down into an alligator bag, he brought up the then-staggering sum of one hundred and eight dollars in cash and paid his bill on the spot.

With the Civil War and Reconstruction in his memory, the American pioneer spirit in his blood, and the overarching strains of Victorian and Southern sensibilities in his upbringing, from 1898 until his death in 1911, W. M. was the right man in the right place doing the right thing in Miami. And yet, in a city known for wild speculation and a boom-and-bust mentality, he was also a calm force in business and the community. Slow and steady, he knew how to win the race. His life prepared him for success. Time after time, he showed that he was a survivor. During the course of his lifetime, he saw his whole way of life disappear. He lost his freedom. He lost a wife and two children. He lost a major business venture, but he never lost his faith in himself. He was daring and resourceful. W. M. lived in a world of infinite possibility and never lost his ability to recognize and to capitalize upon opportunity.

William Murrah Burdine grew up and lived his life in small-town America, where everybody knew his name and where he knew theirs. He was directly affected by some of the largest sweeps of the history of his time. He never sat on the sidelines. He was resilient. He conditioned himself to make the best out of the disruptions and dislocations of day-to-day living.

There was a certain symmetry to his life. No matter where he was, he raised his family, practiced his religion, pursued his business and commercial interests, and consistently supported the advancement of education. Most of all, he

Burdines Archives

The First Burdines on 12th Street (now Flagler) about 1900

The two-story building with the awning is Burdines on 12th Street as it looked at about the turn of the century — complete with horse-drawn carriages and bicycles in the street.

The name W. M. Burdine on the wall is partially obscured by the palm tree.

By 1900, it was clear that 12th Street (now Flagler) would become the main street of the central business district. So, W. M. wasted no time moving his store.

never forgot who he was. Although his journey to Miami took his lifetime, during those years he never lost his Mississippi magic and, because of that, everybody has a Burdines story to tell.

Like his father, who at eighteen had had to grow up fast because of the Civil War, Roddey could not stay young for long. In 1911, when he was only twenty-five, upon the death of his father, he became president of Burdines and was thrust overnight into the stewardship of the family business and assets.

Roddey Burdine's vision was "the good life." He had lived it and was motivated by selling the merchandise of the good life to his customers. He had all the poise, finesse, and daring of a second-generation entrepreneur.

Dubbed "The Merchant Prince" even during his lifetime, Roddey, the most successful of all Burdines, was also in some ways the least likely in his youth to show the promise of what became indisputably a legendary career. As he himself told it, his introduction into the business was swift, rather comical, and anything but auspicious.

Suspended from school for talking back to his teacher, the younger Burdine decided that he would go sailing with a friend instead of going home, where he would have had to explain himself. As luck would have it, their boat capsized. After they were rescued, Roddey still delayed facing the music at home.

That evening, W. M. caught up with his son in a poolroom. As Roddey crawled up on the pool table preparing to make a shot, his father dragged him off by the ear, announcing that the next day Roddey was going to work. By 6 a.m., he was sweeping out the store. For some time, the future

Historical Museum of Southern Florida

Burdines, Spring 1913

Inside the Burdines' "skyscraper," one year after it was opened, the store was filled with an assortment of men's and ladies' hats, stockings and socks, umbrellas, handerkerchiefs, fabrics, lotions and toiletries, dresses, and numerous other items.

The slightly blurred young man in the lower righthand corner looks very much like Roddey Burdine, Sr., who in 1911 became president of Burdines upon the death of his father.

president of Burdines would be restricted to using his talents to wash windows and complete other basic chores under his father's watchful eye.

Recognizing the need to channel his son's youthful energy, W. M. tamed Roddey's exuberance, involving him in the business early on. Eventually, he was allowed to try sales and, still later, buying — in the shoe department, a responsibility which he apparently pursued with such gusto that they never could sell all of their inventory.

Under his father's careful and measured tutelage, it became almost inevitable that R. B. would rise to the challenge of making the family business into a modern, progressive, and enviable corporation. As time would prove, father would lay the groundwork; his son would build the superstructure.

As soon as he became president of Burdines, Roddey took Miami by storm. He was out to prove that he was his own man. Immediately, he showed not only that he was equal to the job, but that he was "a great merchant," "an astute businessman," "a great showman," a born marketer, a natural leader, "a keen judge of human nature," and a man with a special vision. His father had taken the risk of moving south to begin the family business. At less than half his father's age, in 1912, a year after he became president of Burdines, Roddey already scored a major victory.

The symbol of R.B.'s contribution to Burdines is the skyscraper — the five-story department store that he built on Flagler Street in downtown Miami. Then the tallest building in the city, it changed Burdines, Flagler Street, and Roddey Burdine. Roddey borrowed $14,000 to build the

Historical Museum of Southern Florida

Burdines, Downtown Miami
1920's and 30's

By April, 1926, Burdines had expanded into more than half a city block at the northeast corner of South Miami Avenue and First Street, a far cry from the tiny trading post in which W. M. Burdine had first opened for business. Trolleys and cars have replaced horse-drawn wagons and bicycles in the street.

$65,000 building, had an elevator installed, the first in a retail store, and created a sensation.

No longer a cutup adolescent, R. B., had established his reputation as a pacesetter. Because of Burdine's skyscraper, other merchants decided to move to Flagler Street, which became the heart of Miami's retail district.

In fact, the expansiveness that would characterize Roddey Burdine's approach to life and business was apparent early on. Debonair and self-confident, R. B. saw growth as the natural progression of his business, and he was not about to let anyone or anything stand in his way. When Roddey's brother Freeman, an attorney and Burdine corporate officer, objected to the plans for the skyscraper, Roddey told him that he had not come to see him for advice but to have the necessary papers drawn up to facilitate the expansion. "Attorneys have only to know the law," he said. "Merchants must have brains."

R. B. was a stickler for details, at the same time that he was a master of the broad stroke or concept. He made sure that the shoelaces on every manikin were tied, but he also had a natural instinct for the larger challenge of creating an organization in which everyone knows that he or she truly plays an important part. "One of the first things a man has to learn in business," he said, "is how little he can do by himself and that when he finds this out, he begins to look around for people to do what he can't." He knew the names and personal histories of virtually every employee, from the lowest to the highest in the organizational scale, and each felt as though they had not just an employer, but a friend in Roddey Burdine.

Early on under R. B.'s direction, the Burdine clientele began

Reprinted with permission of The Miami Herald

Roddey Bell Burdine died on February 15, 1936

Roddey Burdine's death was front-page news. Few people other than family and close associates knew that his condition had turned grave. So, it was a shocked Miami that heard the rumors and then read the headlines that, at just 49 years of age, R. B. had died of brain fever. The city literally closed during the funeral. In one of the largest funerals in Miami history, community leaders, as well as ordinary citizens, filled the church to overflowing and lined the streets.

to change and diversify. When the store added a fancy goods department for ladies, according to one account, "the Indians in their brilliant calicos now mixed with the first of the blue-serge 'winter visitors,' who came for New Year's and stayed through Washington's Birthday, spending the season, rocking on the yellow and white veranda of the Hotel Royal Palm and shopping for lighter wardrobes at Burdines."

By 1928, Roddey Burdine sent his first buyers to Europe. In 1929, he was advertising in national magazines and telling potential tourists and customers coming to Miami to "bring your trunks empty." It was then that the theme, "Sunshine Fashions," was developed, firmly positioning Burdines as a source of fashion, not only in Miami but nationwide.

Just as the small 25' x 50' trading post that W. M. opened on Avenue D was superseded by a modest, yet larger, facility on 12th Street, the first building on 12th Street was, in turn, overshadowed by Miami's first skyscraper. Eventually, Burdines outgrew even that facility and gobbled up the property to its west and south — until the store occupied the better part of one city block and even spilled over into another.

In addition, as Miami Beach developed, Burdines expanded across the bay, first opening a shop in the Roney Plaza Hotel on Collins Avenue in 1929 and then a branch on fashionable Lincoln Road in 1936. Under Roddey Burdine's leadership, as early as 1925, Burdines had "the biggest volume of retail business in the southeastern states" and had become a legend in retail history.

On February 17, 1936, the City of Miami shut down.

Government offices and businesses were closed. The Miami Chamber of Commerce was draped in black. A shocked city precipitously had gone into mourning. Two days before, Roddey Burdine, first citizen of Miami and president of Burdines, suddenly had died at forty-nine after a brief illness.

At first, no one could believe the rumors. As one newspaper writer observed, "The dreary skies which dripped with rain throughout the day seemed but to reflect the paralysis into which Miami had descended." At Burdines, "curtains were drawn over most of the display windows" and "large funeral wreaths hung on the doors of the three main entrances." Even after two days of front-page banner headlines repeated the news, many people could not face the reality of their loss. As though going through the motions of a ritual they could not understand, a grieving city gathered to pay tribute to "the Merchant Prince."

As the funeral cortege made its way through the streets of the city, it was apparent to everyone that not just the Burdine family, but all of Miami had suffered an irreplaceable loss: "The city's first citizen was dead, and there was none to take his place."

To everyone who knew him, Roddey Burdine had come to symbolize someone who at best comes once in a generation: a person perfectly matched to his time and place, someone who captures the imagination of everyone he meets, and a man who mysteriously raises the level of everyone and everything with which he comes in contact. Roddey Burdine's rare blend of personal presence and genuine compassion made everyone feel better for being around him. He had become a legend in his own time and had brought his family name to heights that no one could have imagined just a few decades before.

But perhaps more than anything else, Roddey Burdine had come to embody the unique promise and opportunity of the young City of Miami, in which he had spent the best years of his youth — a city as eager to prove itself as he had been to display his own natural talents and abilities. R. B.'s accomplishments, as well as those of this family, created and validated the fairytale myths that surrounded the city that they had helped to build. So, at the sudden death of Roddey Burdine, in mid-February, 1936, it seemed to everyone that a certain innocence and insouciance would be lost, possibly forever.

After the death of Roddey Burdine in 1936, his brother, William, Jr., succeeded him as president of Burdines. A recluse who marched to the tune of no audible drummer, he was the least equipped of all the family members to run the business. R. B. had tried without success to get "Willie" interested in the stores; but he was happier in the Everglades among the Indians who took care of his cattle.

Eventually, Willie was elevated to the largely ceremonial position of Chairman of the Board, so that he would do no lasting damage to the family fortune. In 1943, for the first time in its forty-five-year history, a non-family member, George Whitten, the employee of longest standing and Roddey Burdine's righthand man, became president of Burdines.

During the 1940's and 1950's, Burdines expanded and continued its success. Sales in 1898 had been $2,600; in the store's 50th year, they had grown to $25 million. The 25-foot frontage, 1,250 interior, and open space of W. M.'s first store had become the better part of two city blocks, spanning 1,130 feet fronting on three streets with an inside floor space of just under one-half a million square feet. There were seventy-six departments. W. M.'s two paid employees had grown to 3300. Burdines capitalized on the growth of Miami and South Florida and retained all of the outward characteristics that had made it great, long after the two key individuals who had put it on the map in the first place.

The indefinable something that only two larger-than-life personalities could bring to Burdines was lost with the passing of both William Murrah Burdine and Roddey Bell, however. Even though their traditions had been carried on admirably, the age of the Burdine pioneers came to an end and the time of the corporate leaders began. In 1956, Burdines passed from family control when it was sold to Federated Department Stores, ending its 58 years as an independent, family-owned business.

Burdines grew because of the unique ways in which William M. and his son Roddey perfectly complemented each other during their own stewardships of the business. They both were the perfect men to lead the store in their time. Their two personalities and visions worked through the same vehicle in the same environment to achieve the same end. From trading post to skyscraper, together, they left a unique legacy that grew out of the practical, even harsh, necessities of any successful business, but that also went well beyond the bottom line. They created a business that had heart and soul.

Acknowledgements

This book could not have been written had it not been for the generous assistance that I have received from scores of individuals. Dr. and Mrs. John B. Crum opened the world of W. M. Burdine and the Burdine Family in Bartow to me and shared their time, their research and perspectives, and the warmth of their home. Marty Ramage of Tupelo, Mississippi, talked with me, a total stranger, on the telephone and subsequently opened every door to me in Tupelo and its environs and around the state. Because of him, I was able to confirm my suspicions about the critical role that William Burdine's growing up in Mississippi had on his later life.

Carol Weber and Bill Whiting opened the doors for me to search the files of the Miami Herald library. Rose Klayman looked everywhere for me and found everything I needed. Howard Socol, Carey Watson, and Ron Rodriguez gave me unlimited access to the archives at Burdines. Hanalore Hill specially organized the materials for me.

I give special thanks to all of the people who met with, spoke with, or corresponded with me after learning about my project. They wrote articles about my research to help me uncover even more people who had things to share with me. They jogged their memories about the Burdines, researched their personal and historical collections, and even made their unique treasures available to me: Lillian O'Brien, Frank Peterson, Jr., Betsy Robbins, Melissa Curry, Elsie W. Gordon, Grace E. Jones, W. D. Anderson, Joan Fleischman, Phyllis Harper, Jean McNamee, Hugh and Freddie Wright, Nancy Grissom, Joyce Lofton, Julia Roebuck, Clara Marshall, Sandy Watkins, Bill and Marge

McKinney, Doug Carroll, Verna Mae Carroll, Ira McCullen, Jr., Lillian Minga, Jo Uptain-Evans, Kathy Bailey, R. T. Wax, The Lee County Library (Mississippi), Jay Kinzer-Halcrow, Jo Werne, Dan Hobby and Sue Gillis (Fort Lauderdale Historical Society), Joan Morris (Photographic Collection, Florida State Archives), The Mississippi Department of Archives and History, The staff of the Historical Museum of Southern Florida, Dr. Louis E. Knight, Thomas D. Anderson, Patsy Howell, Carol Getz, Dorothy Blau, Virginia G. Falkner, Martha Mercer Hatteson, Joyce Beck, Jerry Goodman, Jack Coleman, Dr. Jack Seitlin, Toni Montilla, Harold Forshey, Robert Fewell, Mason Jackson, Rosalind Collins, Kerry Kennedy (The Orange County Historical Museum), Fran Desmond, Donald J. Ivey (Pinellas County Historical Museum), Beth Boggs (Maitland Historical Society, Inc.), Tish Davies (Florida Adventure Museum), Joseph Spann (Polk County Historical and Genealogical Library), Donna Jean Hayes (Lake County Historical Society), Mary Virginia Mealey (Depot Museum), Yolanda A. Conrow (West Pasco Society, Inc.), Wanda Bell Edwards (Halifax Historical Society, Inc.), Peggy McCall (Boca Raton Historical Society, Inc.), Samuel Proctor (Oral History Program, University of Florida), Mary Dorsey (Citrus County, Historical Resources Office), Linda R. Steffee (Osceola County Historical Society and Museum), Patricia Bartlett (Matheson Historical Center), Sara Van Arsdel (Orange County Historical Society, Inc.).

Bibliographic Note

Most of the information on the Burdine family and Burdines is contained in numerous newspaper and periodical references. Three longer studies are worthy of mention. Roberta Morgan's *"It's Better at Burdines: How the Famous Store Grew Hand in Hand with Florida"* (The Pickering Press, Miami, 1991) focuses on Burdines' corporate history within the context of a developing Miami and South Florida. Its scope extends well beyond the time that Burdines was a family-owned enterprise. Dr. Paul S. George's unpublished manuscript, "The Burdine Family: An American Saga," contains information on William Murrah Burdine, Sr. and Roddey Bell Burdine, Sr. and other Burdine family members not associated with the family business enterprise. Dr. George also contributed a chapter, "William M. Burdine: Pioneering Miami Merchant and Civic Leader," to *Florida Pathfinders*, ed. Lewis N. Wynne and James J. Horgan (St. Leo College Press, 1994), which discusses the life and business acumen of William M. Burdine, Sr.

New from the

SUCCESS ⬤ SERIES

50 Ways to Get Promoted

Nathan G. Jensen

Tear Down Limits! Stomp Out Mediocrity! Get Innovative!

Introducing *50 Ways to Get Promoted*, an inspiring guide written to snap you out of your workplace-rut and to challenge you to become a shining star — regardless of the type of work you do. It explains the basic principles that can help you get promoted in your workplace by using examples that make clear, logical sense.

50 Ways to Get Promoted includes chapters such as:
Become Visible • Work Smart • Think Big, Be Big!
• Don't Brown-Nose • Overcome Politics • Become Passionate •
• Abandon the Status Quo • Make Your Promotion a No-Brainer •
Forget Past Failures • Speak Up in Meetings • Become a Michelangelo • Create a Blueprint for Your Career

50 Ways to Get Promoted
Nathan G. Jensen
ISBN: 1-55571-506-0
Paperback: $10.95
Order Direct at 1-800-228-2275

Also available from
The Oasis Press®
The Leading Publisher of Small Business Information

Before You Go Into Business, Read This

Ira N. Nottonson

business basics for those too embarrassed to ask

Running a business is about knowing the rules of the game. *Before You Go Into Business, Read This* does not pretend to paint the yellow brick road. It is designed to help the business person read the signposts of danger and recognize the most successful business strategies in a simple, easy to understand format. It offers both practical and philosophical approaches to business that work and are easy to apply to your self-employment aspirations!

Before You Go Into Business, Read This
Ira N. Nottonson
ISBN: 1-55571-481-1
Paperback: $17.95
Order Direct at 1-800-228-2275

Also available from
The Oasis Press®
The Leading Publisher of Small Business Information

Renaissance 2000

Luigi Salvaneschi

Liberal Arts Essentials for Tomorrow's Leaders

Carving a niche for yourself and developing a successful career has never been more difficult. *Renaissance 2000* shows how drawing off liberal arts disciplines can lead to better perception and communication skills, incisive and integrated thought processes, or a deeper understanding of players in the global marketplace — all necessary to stay competitive in your business or industry.

Each chapter focuses on an aspect of the liberal arts and provides exercises and references to help you become an insightful and inspired visionary for the new millennium.

Ideal for anyone who wants to break away from the pack.

Renaissance 2000
Luigi Salvaneschi
ISBN: 1-55571-412-9
Paperback Success Series: $22.95
Order Direct at 1-800-228-2275

Also available from
The Oasis Press®
The Leading Publisher of Small Business Information

SmartStart Your (State) Business

The only up-to-date, state-specific startup guide of its kind

You may be like more than 35 million other Americans that dream of owning their own business. If fact, there has never been a better time to start a small business. *SmartStart Your (State) Business* goes beyond other business how-to books and provides you with:

- **Quick references to the most current federal, state, local and private agencies that will help your business get up and running;**
- **State-specific issues that you'll need to consider before starting your business**
- **Methods to develop a powerful marketing strategy, create a favorable public relations plan, and confidently price your product or service.**
- **Guidelines to write a smart and functional business plan (includes a sample plan)**
- **Plus several other key business elements to consider**

SmartStart Your (State) Business
ISBN: varies per state
Paperback: $19.95
Order Direct at 1-800-228-2275

Order Directly from
The Oasis Press®
The Leading Publisher of Small Business Information

We are proud to offer one of the most diverse and comprehensive business libraries on the market today. For over 20 years, The Oasis Press® has been dedicated to helping small businesses grow. Our philosophy of providing this kind of "nuts and bolts" information has taken our business from a two-person operation in a Texas garage to its standing as the leading publisher of small business information today. If you would like to receive a free product catalog or find a book on a particular subject, give us a call.

Order Direct at
1-800-228-2275
or visit our Web site at:
http://www.psi-research.com/oasis.htm